DISCARD

Building
Decks

PRO TIPS AND SIMPLE STEPS

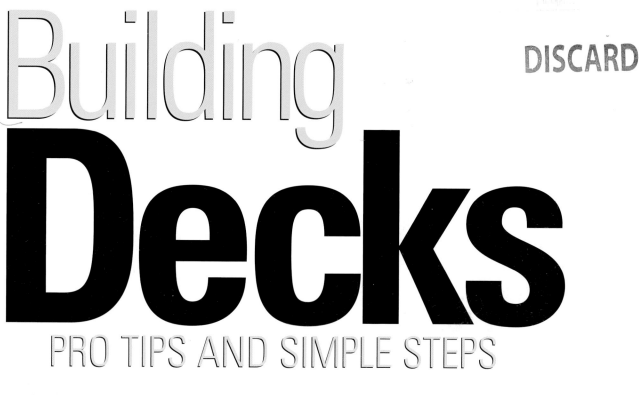

Meredith® Books
Des Moines, Iowa

Stanley® Books
An imprint of Meredith® Books

Stanley Building Decks
Editor: Ken Sidey
Senior Associate Design Director: Tom Wegner
Assistant Editor: Harijs Priekulis
Copy Chief: Terri Fredrickson
Copy and Production Editor: Victoria Forlini
Editorial Operations Manager: Karen Schirm
Managers, Book Production: Pam Kvitne,
    Marjorie J. Schenkelberg
Technical Editors, The Stanley Works: Mike Maznio,
    Jim Olson
Contributing Copy Editor: Jim Stepp
Technical Proofreader: Tom Garcia
Contributing Proofreaders: Becky Danley, Raymond L. Kast,
    Debra Morris Smith
Electronic Production Coordinator: Paula Forest
Editorial and Design Assistant: Renee E. McAtee,
    Kathleen Stevens

**Additional Editorial Contributions from
    Greenleaf Publishing**
Publishing Director: Dave Toht
Writer: Steve Cory
Art Director: Rebecca Anderson
Designer: Jean DeVaty
Contributing Editor: David Schiff
Editorial Assistant: Betony Toht
Illustrator: Dave Brandon
Photography: Dan Stultz, Stultz Photography

Meredith® Books
Editor in Chief: James D. Blume
Design Director: Matt Strelecki
Managing Editor: Gregory H. Kayko
Executive Editor, Gardening and Home Improvement:
    Benjamin W. Allen
Executive Editor, Home Improvement: Larry Erickson

Director, Sales, Special Markets: Rita McMullen
Director, Sales, Premiums: Michael A. Peterson
Director, Sales, Retail: Tom Wierzbicki
Director, Book Marketing: Brad Elmitt
Director, Operations: George A. Susral
Director, Production: Douglas M. Johnston

Vice President and General Manager: Douglas J. Guendel

Meredith Publishing Group
President, Publishing Group: Stephen M. Lacy
Vice President-Publishing Director: Bob Mate

Meredith Corporation
Chairman and Chief Executive Officer: William T. Kerr

Chairman of the Executive Committee: E.T. Meredith III

Thanks to
Jeffrey and Sherri Kreafle
Scott and Diana Moore
Jay and Janice Wood
The Deck Yard

All of us at Stanley® Books are dedicated to providing you with the
information and ideas you need to enhance your home and garden.
We welcome your comments and suggestions about this book.
Write to us at:
    Meredith Corporation
    Stanley Books
    1716 Locust St.
    Des Moines, IA 50309–3023

If you would like more information on other Stanley products,
call 1-800-STANLEY or visit us at: www.stanleyworks.com
Stanley® and the notched rectangle around the Stanley name are
registered trademarks of The Stanley Works and subsidiaries.

If you would like to purchase any of our home improvement,
cooking, crafts, gardening, or home decorating and design books,
check wherever quality books are sold. Or visit us at:
meredithbooks.com

690.184

CONTENTS

FREESTANDING DECK WITH PLANTERS AND BENCHES

A deck with a simple shape and straightforward design complements almost any home style. This design adds planters and a bench to set it a step above the plain rectangular decks often attached to homes.

Low-cost, easy to build

Several features make this design easy to build. The joists overhang the beam, so the posts and beam do not have to be precisely positioned. The hefty beam needs fewer piers—a real worksaver, since digging and setting piers can be the most difficult stage of deck building.

The large beam also permits a 3-foot cantilever. That's important for new homes where the backfill dirt along the foundation has not settled: building codes often require piers to be set as deep as 8 feet. The longer cantilever allows piers to be set farther away from the backfill, so they need not be as deep. The rectangular shape allows joists to be cut the same length. Angled decking adds visual appeal and requires only a bit more care than straight decking to install.

This deck uses pressure-treated lumber for all its parts. Treated wood is inexpensive and resistant to rot, and it can be stained to mimic cedar or redwood.

Getting the size right

The upper level, minus the benches and planters, is 10×12 feet, allowing plenty of room for a grill, a food prep table, and a pathway. The lower level is roughly 14 feet square, a good size for a dining area. If you vary the design, check *pages 20–21* to make sure you provide enough space for seating and activities, as well as a lane for traffic.

Massive beams made of three 2×10s rest on 6×6 posts, which in turn rest on 12-inch-diameter footings. These larger-than-usual elements allow the beam to overhang the footings by 3 feet. On most sites, a beam made of double 2×8s resting on 4×4s and 10-inch footings would suffice.

A bench made of 2×4 pieces is supported at each end by cleats attached to planters. Middle support posts are made of 4×4s; the bench top is ⁵⁄₄×6 decking.

The planter walls are made of ⁵⁄₄×6 decking pieces held together with cleats. Trim pieces made of decking ripped down the middle finish the corners. A shelf inside the planter holds the plant container.

This two-level deck eases the transition from the kitchen/family room to the yard. A simple step fits under the deeply cantilevered deck. The entire deck is made from pressure-treated lumber.

DECK ON A SLOPED SITE WITH RAILING AND STAIRS

This is a basic rectangular deck with two twists: An angle is cut out of one corner for a stairway, and the site is sloped, making for some challenging framing work.

Size and shape
This deck is 14×24 feet, providing ample room for a food preparation area, a dining area, and a lounge chair or two. The rectangular shape allows several options for positioning outdoor furniture.

The structure
The deck is attached to the house with a ledger board. Installing a ledger reduces the number of footings, posts, and beams required, saving time and work. A ledger installed at the beginning of construction also provides a handy reference point when laying out the deck. However, installing a ledger

board creates its own challenges (see *pages 58–61*).

Concrete footings support 4×4 posts, which in turn support beams made of doubled 2×10s. A long beam supports most of the deck. A shorter beam, placed at an angle, is needed for the cutoff corner.

The framing is mostly 2×10 joists attached with joist hangers. The angled corner is not difficult to make.

Stairs and railing
This popular railing design uses standard dimensional lumber: 4×4 posts, 2×2 balusters, 2×4 rails, and a top cap of decking. The only difficult joint is where top cap pieces meet at a corner, requiring a mitered cut.

The stairway descends about 4 feet. *Pages 73–75* offer detailed instructions on planning and building stairs.

The beam is made of doubled 2×10s and rests on top of posts. Special hardware anchors each post to its footing and the beam to the post.

A divider strip on the nearly 24×14-foot deck allows for the use of two 12-foot decking pieces instead of longer, more expensive pieces. Other than at this strip, no joints were necessary in the decking.

This railing is one of the most common designs, using 4×4 posts, 2×4 top and bottom rails, 2×2 balusters, and a 2×6 top cap. Newels attached directly above each post add a simple decorative touch.

Built to cope with a steep slope on a shallow backyard, this deck features a stairway that angles off one corner. The simple but appealing railing treatment blends with the traditional style house.

TWO-LEVEL DECK WITH WIDE STAIRS AND A PERGOLA

This two-tier design starts by using ideas from the first two decks in this book and adds several custom features. It will take longer to build than the other designs, but none of the elements requires advanced woodworking skills.

Angled decking

On the upper level, the angled decking adds a custom look that is easy to achieve. Decking pieces run at 45-degree angles to a center strip. If the angled pieces were to butt against each other, the joints would have to be perfect. But the center strip allows the deck to look great without requiring perfect cuts.

As long as the center strip is positioned accurately, most of the decking pieces will be exactly the same size, so they can be cut rapidly.

Spacious stairs

The stairs are 8 feet wide and 14 inches deep. Such spacious dimensions allow the stairs to double as seating, especially handy for entertaining large groups. The landing at the bottom of the stairs, made of patio pavers set on a sand bed, creates a graceful transition from deck to yard.

Railing and pergola

This railing design uses more components than the simpler design shown on *pages 80–83*, but it is not difficult to build. The posts and railing sections can be prefabricated to produce a neater final product.

The pergola, a simple overhead lattice, provides space for hanging plants and a privacy screen. Like the skirt around the base of the deck, it is made from vinyl lattice.

Supported by posts made of 2×4s and 1×4s, a balustrade made of 2×2 balusters and 2×4 rails spans from post to post. ⁵⁄₄×6 decking is used for the rail cap. The balusters have alternating spacing of 1½ and 3½ inches.

To assure a solid railing, posts are lag-bolted to the header and outside joists. Vinyl lattice skirting, trimmed with pressure-treated 1×4s, covers the area beneath the deck. Corner posts use three 2×4s and one 1×4.

The pergola is an attention-grabbing feature that is surprisingly simple to build. Four 4×4 posts support 2×8 beams and 2×6 rafters, which are topped off with 2×2s. Lattice sections span between the posts.

This deck features two levels, wide entry stairs, a chevron decking pattern, lattice skirting, and an overhead pergola, but is still fundamentally simple to construct.

GETTING READY

Compared to many home remodeling projects, deck building is easy and enjoyable. It is outdoor work. It involves simple materials, and it won't disrupt everyday home life as other remodeling projects do. It's not a problem to leave the work half-finished and pick up where you left off several days later.

No building job, however, including a deck, should be approached haphazardly. Good decisions at the planning stage can save hassles later on, so be willing to spend as much time in preparing as in actually building a deck.

Making plans
Start by walking around the site and making rough sketches. Note especially the patterns of sun and shade, views worth preserving, and likely foot-traffic patterns. Gradually refine the drawings, and consult with your local building department to make sure that your plans comply with local codes. *Pages 20–27* walk you through the process.

Choosing tools and materials
Assemble the kit of carpentry hand tools shown at right. Most of these tools are useful for many household projects. They will be handy to have around the house long after the deck is finished, so invest in high quality tools. Avoid bargain-bin, off-brand tools, which often break or bend easily and typically are less comfortable to use. *Pages 12–13* discuss the required power tools.

Decide on the type of lumber and then select boards with an eye to quality. *Pages 14–17* explain how.

To check for level over long distances, use a carpenter's level atop a straight board, a line level, or a water level.

Line level

Mason's line

Water level

An inexpensive post level makes setting posts much easier. It allows hands-free work, and it indicates whether a post is plumb in both directions.

For a successful project, choose the right tools and materials and draw detailed plans.

CHAPTER PREVIEW

Power tools
page 12

Selecting framing lumber
page 14

Choosing deck and railing materials
page 15

Selecting boards
page 16

T-bevel

A 25- or 30-foot, 1-inch-wide tape measure is an all-purpose measuring

Hand sander

Use a layout square to quickly mark for 90- and 45-degree cuts. It can also be used to mark other angles.

Carpenter's pencil

Pry bar

Cordless drill

Tool belt

Chalk line

Ratchet and socket

Carpenter's square

Squeeze clamp

Chisel

Bar clamp

Most homeowners prefer a 16-ounce hammer; a 20-ounce one packs a wallop but requires a strong arm.

Sledge

Nail set

Clamshell digger

Handsaw

Choosing fasteners
page 18

Designing for beauty and utility
page 20

Making sure it's strong
page 22

Building an above-average deck
page 24

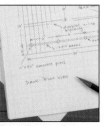

Drawing a plan
page 26

Basic skills
page 28

POWER TOOLS

If you already own some of the tools shown on these pages, test their quality before beginning a deck project. If you have difficulty cutting a straight line or boring a hole, try a new blade or bit. If the tool still is a struggle to use, buy a new one that will produce clean lines with ease.

The three most common power tools—circular saw, saber saw, and drill—are all you need for most deck work. Here's what to look for:

Power saws

A smooth-running **circular saw** equipped with a sharp blade will cut through lumber with ease and precision. Choose a saw that uses a 7¼-inch blade. The saw should pull at least 13 amps (1560 watts) and run on ball and/or needle bearings. Pick up the saw and handle it—it should feel comfortable in your grip. The knobs to adjust the cutting angle should be easy to use; make sure you can easily sight down the guide on the baseplate as you cut.

A 40-tooth **carbide-tipped circular saw blade** cuts rough lumber with ease and produces a fine, splinter-free edge.

A **saber saw,** sometimes called a jigsaw, is designed to cut curves. A cheap saber saw will cut slowly and wobble, producing an uneven line. Choose a model with a large, solid baseplate that will stay firmly in place during cutting. The saw should pull at least 4.5 amps (540 watts) and run on ball and/or needle bearings. A sawdust blower is a useful feature: It clears the guide line of sawdust as you make the cut.

Purchase several **saber saw blades** because they break easily. For most deck work, use medium- or heavy-duty blades, designed to cut through 2×s.

Power drills

If you plan to attach decking with screws, you will need a **power drill**. A cheap drill will burn out under the load. Use a ⅜-inch, reversing and variable-speed drill that pulls at least 3 amps (360 watts). A cordless drill is handy but will drive screws more slowly than a corded drill. For deck work, a cordless drill should use at least 14 volts. Use two rechargeable batteries so one can charge while the other is in use.

Drill bits become dull quickly, especially

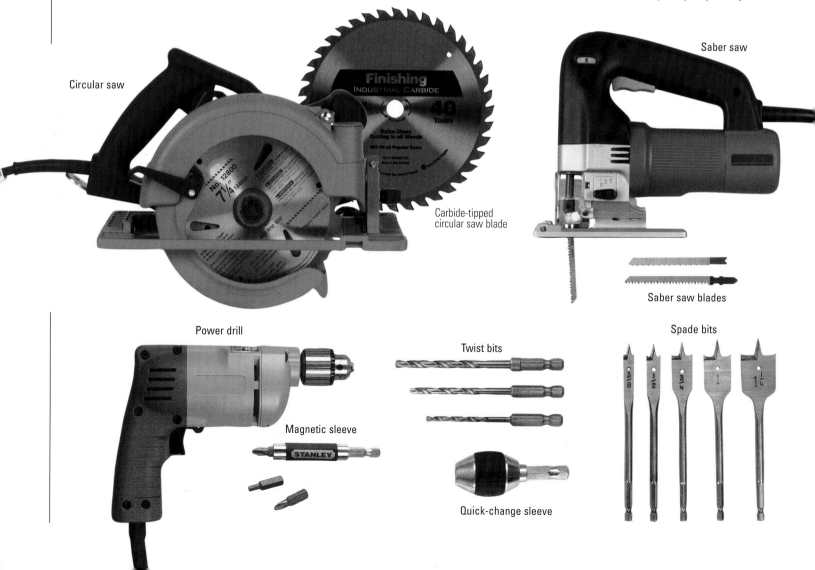

Circular saw

Saber saw

Carbide-tipped circular saw blade

Saber saw blades

Power drill

Twist bits

Spade bits

Magnetic sleeve

Quick-change sleeve

if they hit a nail. Buy a complete set of **twist bits.** "Titanium" bits last longer than cheaper bits. You may also need **spade bits** of several sizes. **Quick-change** and **magnetic sleeves** are time-savers.

Optional tools

Some tools may make the work go faster, and they help achieve a more professional look to the deck. For seldom-used tools, consider renting rather than buying; a rented tool may be of higher quality than one you buy.

A **power miter saw,** commonly called a chop saw, makes precise cuts of any angle. To make 45-degree cuts through a 2×6 (or 5⁄4×6 decking), you'll need a model with at least a 12-inch blade. A compound miter feature is not needed for deck work.

A quick way to give railings and deck edges a custom look is to go over them with a **router.** Use a self-guiding bit, which runs along the edge of the material and virtually prevents mistakes. A roundover bit produces a radius edge.

When you're attaching a ledger to a brick, block, or concrete surface, a **hammer drill** can reduce labor dramatically. With the "hammer" feature on, it attacks the surface with hammerlike pulsations while it drills.

A **nail gun** drives a nail instantly with the pull of a trigger and can speed up a job. Different guns drive different sizes of nails. Most nail guns require a large air compressor. Some models are electrically driven or powered by a gas cartridge and a battery. If you want to use one for decking, experiment on scrap pieces of decking to make sure that the nails will not be driven too deeply.

Rent a power auger if you have several postholes to dig. See *page 38* for instructions on choosing and using a power auger. A cordless screwgun *(page 18)* speeds fastening decking with deck screws. A small concrete mixer *(page 39)* is better than hand mixing if you have many piers to pour. A biscuit joiner *(page 24)* reinforces miter joints in railings.

Router

Power miter saw

PLUNGE ROUTER
TOUPIE DE PLONGEE
TUPI CON EFECTO DE EMBOLO
1³⁄₄ HP

———— Roundover bit

Masonry bit

Nail gun

Hammer drill

SELECTING FRAMING LUMBER

Lumber used for decks must be resistant to rot. Standard lumber, such as pine, fir, or hemlock, will survive only a few years of exposure to most climates. Painting standard lumber is not a good option, because it's hard to cover all the surfaces.

Pressure-treated lumber works best for framing. Infused with a chemical, this type of lumber resists rotting. Some types of wood are less porous than others, so the lumber is cut with a grid of small incisions before being treated. These incisions will not disappear, so don't use this type of lumber where it will be visible. Wood that has been kiln-dried after treatment (KDAT) is the highest quality. "Brown-treated" lumber is just as durable as greenish pressure-treated lumber and has the natural color of stained wood. However, even green pressure-treated lumber can be stained so that it resembles cedar or redwood.

For posts **4×4s** are standard. Cleats and stiffeners are made from **2×4s**. Joists and beams may be **2×6s**, **2×8s**, **2×10s**, or **2×12s**.

4×4   2×4   2×6   2×8   2×10   2×12

STANLEY PRO TIP

Trust pressure treated

Ask dealer for Consumer Info. Sheet.
0.40 pcf   Chromated Copper Arsenate
Ground Contact   CCA-C   AWPA UC4A, C2, C9
LIFETIME LIMITED WARRANTY
Universal Forest Products
Grand Rapids, MI 49525   ✓ TP

Most pressure-treated lumber is infused with chromated copper arsenate (CCA) to make it rot-resistant. Look for a label or stamp that says "ground contact" or gives a CCA rating of 0.40 percent or greater. This ominous-sounding ingredient bonds firmly to the wood fiber, and once the lumber is installed it is safe. But CCA is toxic. Exposed skin that comes into contact with the dust may develop a rash. Inhalation of dust may cause serious illness.

Keep children out of the work area. Wear protective clothing, a dust mask, and safety glasses while working. Sweep up thoroughly and dispose of scraps. Do not burn CCA-treated lumber.

Composite railing components

Wood/plastic composite framing members such as 4×4s, 2×4s, and 2×2s can be used for building railings but are not structurally suitable for the superstructure of the deck.

Lumber sizes

A very old, rough 2×4 may actually measure 2 inches by 4 inches. Today, lumber is smoother and smaller. A board's actual dimensions are less than its "nominal" size in both directions. For instance, a nominal 2×4 is actually 1½ inches by 3½ inches.

Lumber from 2×6s on up can vary as much as ¼ inch in width—even if taken from the same stack at the lumberyard. Posts larger than 4×4 are prone to twists and cracks; consider sandwiching 2×s instead.

CHOOSING DECK AND RAILING MATERIALS

For the deck surface, choose pressure-treated, cedar, or redwood 2×4s, 2×6s, or 5/4×6 decking. The latter, available in cedar and pressure-treated fir, is 1 inch thick and 5½ inches wide with rounded edges for a splinter-free surface.

Pressure-treated decking is the least expensive and the most reliably resistant to rot, but you'll have to choose carefully to get wood that is straight and free of loose knots.

Cedar grades that include the word "Architect" usually are heartwood, the dense centermost core of the tree. Most cedar decking is sapwood (the softer, lighter area of the tree closer to the bark) and must be treated. Cedar 1× lumber usually has one rough side and one smooth side.

Plastic/wood composite and **vinyl** decking is extremely durable and requires almost no maintenance. If the sun will beat on the deck, choose a brand that has proven itself colorfast; many types fade dramatically over the years. Some, but not all, can be stained when they fade.

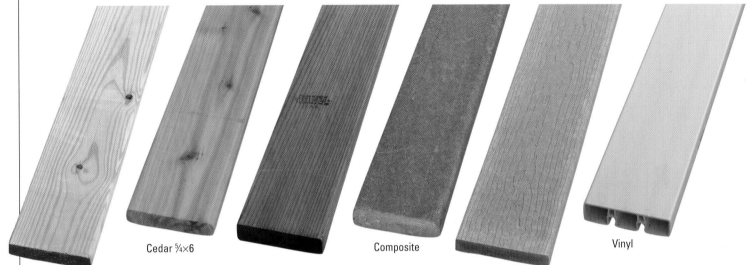

Pressure-treated 5/4×6

Cedar 5/4×6

Redwood 2×6

Composite

Composite with grain

Vinyl

Redwood grades

B-grade

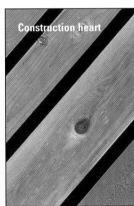

Construction heart

Construction common

"B-grade" redwood has only tiny knots and is all heartwood—a desirable but expensive choice for decking.

Construction heart has knots but no sapwood. **Construction common** has large knots and is partly sapwood.

If you want to retain the brown color of these boards, plan to stain them every year or two; otherwise, allow them to "go gray" *(pages 106–107).*

Light sapwood areas

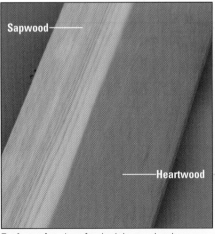

Sapwood

Heartwood

Redwood and **cedar** look better, but be sure the wood will resist rot. If the boards contain light-colored sapwood, they may rot in a few years unless treated regularly with preservative.

SELECTING BOARDS

Perhaps you're lucky enough to have access to a great lumberyard—one that keeps its boards neatly stacked and chooses only the best pieces for its customers. If so, order the lumber for your deck—adding 15 percent for waste—and have them deliver it.

Unfortunately, at most lumber outlets good boards mingle with warped and defective pieces. The only way to get strong and attractive lumber is to pick up the boards one by one, examine each, and choose only those that suit your needs.

Living with imperfection

These days, it's rare to find a board that is completely free of defects. So think about how each board will be used and make sure it is free from *important* defects. For instance, framing lumber that will be hidden needs to be straight and free of major cracks, but it need not be pretty. Decking

and fascia boards need have only one good-looking side. It's OK if some boards are bowed or even a little twisted, because they can be straightened when you install them. Boards used for the railing will be seen from both sides, so they need to be straight and attractive on both sides.

Defects to look for

Here are some common lumber problems:
■ A **crook** is a bend along the length of the board, visible as you sight down its top edge. A slight crook—no more than ¾ inch in an 8-foot board—is not a problem for any board except the top cap of a railing. When a board is installed on edge, a slight crook is sometimes called a crown (below right).
■ A slight corkscrew shape in a board is known as a **twist**. If the twist is noticeable, reject the board.
■ A **check** is a crack that appears on the surface only and is usually only a cosmetic

problem. However, if the crack runs more than halfway through the thickness of a board, reject the board.
■ A short crack running through the thickness of the board at its end is a **split**. If the cracked portion plus an inch or so can be cut off, then accept the board.
■ If a **knot** is larger than 1 inch in diameter, or if it feels loose, it may come out in time. A knot is primarily a cosmetic problem; if it is tight it usually does not affect the strength of the board.
■ A **wane** is a rounded-off corner along the edge of a board, where bark used to be. It is usually only a cosmetic problem, though it slightly reduces a board's nailing surface.
■ A curve across the width of a board is a **cup.** Unless it is severe, cupping is not a problem for framing lumber. In a decking board, slight cupping can be taken out by screwing down each side of the board.

IMPERFECTIONS TO WATCH FOR

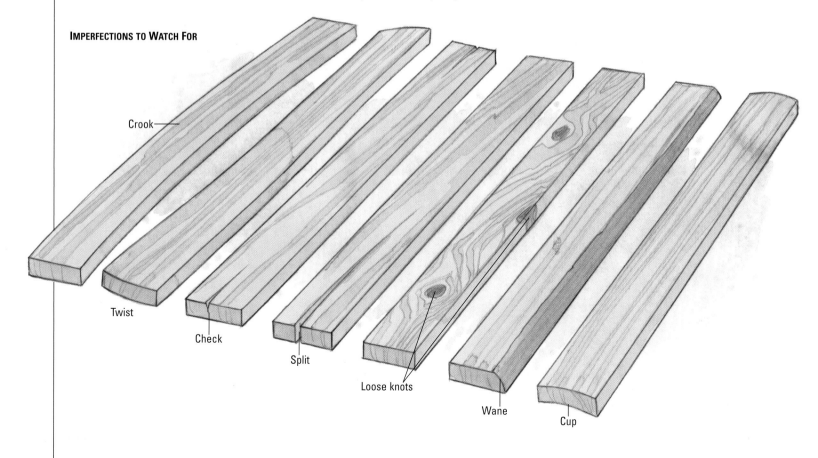

Crook

Twist

Check

Split

Loose knots

Wane

Cup

Vertical and flat grain

Boards with narrow parallel lines, called vertical grain, are stronger and less likely to warp than boards with widely spaced curved lines, called flat grain. Many boards have a mixture of vertical and flat grain. When possible, choose boards with more vertical grain than flat grain.

Sealing cut edges

Cedar and redwood benefit from rot-preventing treatment. In addition, pressure-treating often does not reach the center of a thick board; this means that when the board is cut, untreated wood is exposed. To keep a board from rotting, give the cut edge a quick soak in sealer or apply sealer with a paintbrush. It's usually easier to apply sealer before installing the board.

Examining a board

It takes about 10 seconds to examine a board. Check for twist and crook by picking up one end and sighting down its length. Then examine the sides and edges for defects such as loose knots, cracks, and wane. When using lumber for framing, place the board so that the **crown** (a slight upward crook) is up.

STANLEY PRO TIP

Check for moisture

A board that is wet—either with sap or with pressure treatment—will warp when it dries out unless it is tightly stacked or firmly nailed in place. It will certainly shrink in width and perhaps in length as well.

Consult a board's label to find out its moisture content. "Kiln Dried" is the driest. A board with a moisture content above 15 percent will likely warp unless it is fastened securely.

The label describes a board's moisture content when it left the mill. If a board has been lying around in a lumberyard for months, it may have dried out or become wet. To check a board for moisture, hit it with a hammer. If you see a small spray of liquid or if the indentation feels moist, then the board holds significant moisture.

Wet decking can be installed, but be aware that it will shrink in width. When builders install wet decking, they often leave out spacers (page 51), so the boards are fairly snug against each other. When the boards dry out, ⅛-inch gaps will appear between them.

Once removed from the stack, wet lumber can dry quickly, especially if the weather is dry. If left out in the sun, a loose board may warp in an hour. Keep boards tightly stacked until you use them and then fasten them securely with nails or screws.

CHOOSING FASTENERS

Choose screws, nails, and anchoring hardware that can stand up to many years of moisture. Standard galvanized fasteners have a single coating of protection, which may not be enough if the surface will be rubbed or pounded. Some galvanized nail and screw heads, for example, quickly rust. This not only mars their appearance but also weakens them. "Double-dipped" galvanized fasteners are better protected, but for the best performance buy coated products made specifically for decks.

Nails or screws?

Should the visible portions of the deck be fastened with nails or with screws? Either fastener has its pros and cons.

With the proper tools, screws are nearly as quick and easy to drive as nails, and they hold stronger. As long as they are driven in accurately, without the head stripped, screws are easier to remove than nails if a mistake is made.

However, many people don't like the way screw heads look. A small amount of water will puddle inside a screw head. And if the screw head is stripped, which can easily happen, removing the screw is difficult.

To an experienced builder, driving nails is a bit faster than driving screws. Many people prefer the simple look of nailheads,

and water will not puddle on a nailhead.

On the negative side, if you miss a nail head with the hammer, or if you drive the nail too far—two mistakes that are easy to make—you will mar the wood. And it is difficult to remove a nailed-down board without damaging the board.

Either screws or nails can be used to construct the framing.

Framing fasteners

Use **16d** (16 "penny") **nails** or **3-inch deck screws** to attach 2× lumber. Both hold well, but screws let you redo things more easily in case of a mistake. Check with your building inspector—some codes prohibit

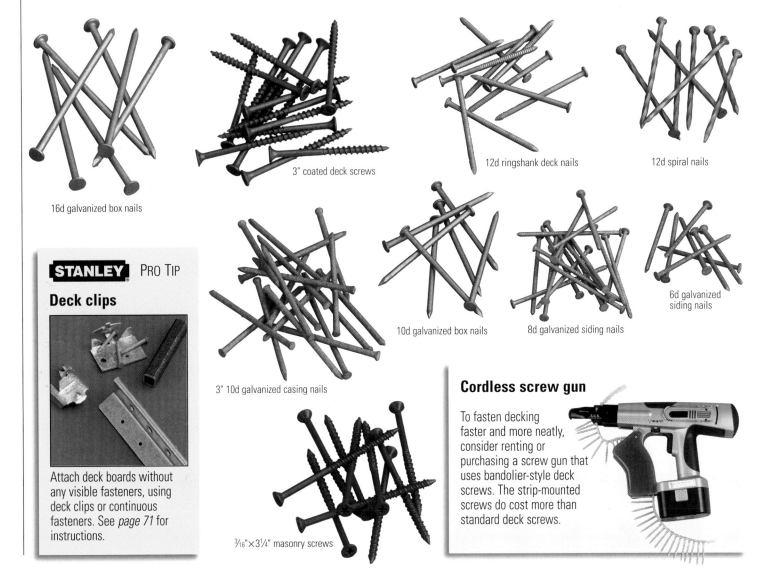

3" coated deck screws

16d galvanized box nails

12d ringshank deck nails

12d spiral nails

10d galvanized box nails

8d galvanized siding nails

6d galvanized siding nails

3" 10d galvanized casing nails

³⁄₁₆"×3¹⁄₄" masonry screws

Deck clips

Attach deck boards without any visible fasteners, using deck clips or continuous fasteners. See *page 71* for instructions.

Cordless screw gun

To fasten decking faster and more neatly, consider renting or purchasing a screw gun that uses bandolier-style deck screws. The strip-mounted screws do cost more than standard deck screws.

screws. Buy screwdriver bits to match the screw head. Bits grab firmer when using square-hole or special deck screw heads rather than a standard phillips head.

For ¾ decking use 2½-inch coated screws or **12d ringshank** or **spiral nails**. The same fasteners can be used for railings. Use **10d, 8d,** and **6d galvanized box** or **casing nails** to attach 1× lumber.

Heavy-duty screws and bolts

To fasten a large piece such as a post, use either a **lag screw** or a **carriage bolt**. Bolts are stronger and can be tightened in future years if the lumber shrinks. Always use washers so that the bolt or screw head does not sink into the wood.

To attach to brick, block, or concrete, use a **lag screw** with a **masonry anchor** (*page 60*). To hold a ledger temporarily, use **masonry screws,** which are not quite as strong but much easier to drive.

Anchoring hardware

Framing members can be joined together using nails or screws, but codes often require special metal hardware pieces for extra-strong joints. Attach joists to the side of a ledger or beam using **joist hangers**. At the corner, either cut a joist hanger in half using tin snips or use an **angle bracket.** Angled joist hangers accommodate joists that attach at a 45-degree angle.

Where a beam sits on top of a post, a **post cap** provides a reliable joint. If joists sit on top of a beam, many local codes allow you simply to angle-drive screws to secure the joists to the beam. Other local building departments require special **hurricane** (or "seismic") **ties,** which add lateral strength.

A **post anchor** secures a post to a concrete pier and supports it so the bottom can dry between rainfalls. Some types are adjustable, in case you make a small error.

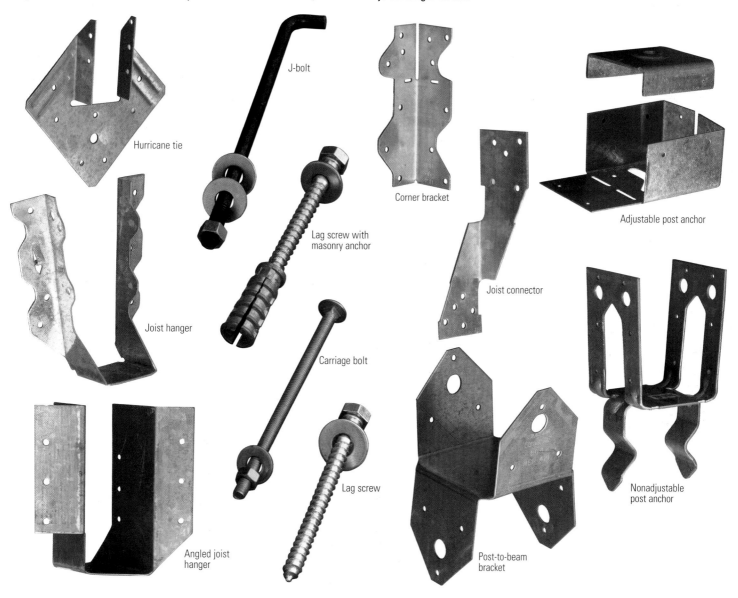

Hurricane tie

J-bolt

Corner bracket

Adjustable post anchor

Joist hanger

Lag screw with masonry anchor

Joist connector

Carriage bolt

Angled joist hanger

Lag screw

Post-to-beam bracket

Nonadjustable post anchor

DESIGNING FOR BEAUTY AND UTILITY

List all the activities you foresee happening on your deck: lounging, barbecuing, entertaining, soaking in a spa, container gardening, storing gear, and more. In your design, try to accommodate as many of these activities as possible.

Size and shape

Unless you expect to entertain large groups, there's little need for a huge deck. Just make sure you have ample space for all the activity areas you need (see *page 21*).

A rectangular deck provides the most available space, and a simple shape may be the most attractive design. But don't be afraid to add an angle or two. An octagonal shape accommodates a round table nicely. Simple 45-degree angles add visual interest, often without sacrificing usable space.

Consider dividing the deck into two or more sections: one area for lounging and another for dining and cooking. Orient one section at a different angle, or use planters or steps to create a transition between the two areas.

A deck doesn't have to be right next to the house. A peninsula or even an island of natural wood offers a pleasant retreat from daily life.

Situating a deck for comfort

As you plan your deck, note the sun and wind patterns in your yard. Situate the dining area in evening shade. Provide a lounging area with part shade and part sun. If you have strong winds, use plantings or a fence to minimize the gusts.

Plan amenities

Don't neglect the add-ons that make a deck more than just an outdoor floor. An overhead structure or trellis provides shade as well as a setting for climbing plants. A high railing with lattice panels provides privacy and screens undesirable views.

Built-in planters and benches unify different areas of a deck. You may prefer large flowerpots and attractive patio furniture, which can be moved to suit the occasion. If so, allow space for them in your plan.

Plan for lighting as well. Low-voltage lights are inexpensive and easy to install, and can be mounted around the deck. You may also need brighter standard-voltage lights and an electrical receptacle or two. Consult with an electrician about adding those features.

Design with views in mind

Keep three views in mind: The way the deck looks to passersby, what you see when you are sitting on the deck, and the view from inside the house.

■ **The view from the street:** Though a deck is primarily a horizontal surface, passersby and neighbors see the vertical elements—railings, steps, benches, overhead structures, planters, and skirting. If the deck has few vertical elements, budget for some lawn furniture and flowerpots.

■ **The view from the deck:** If the deck overlooks a beautiful view—be it

a magnificent hillside or a lovely yard—orient the deck so that people can get a good look while they are sitting on benches or chairs. If you have small children, make sure you won't have to strain to see them while they play in the yard.

■ **The view from inside:** If you have a cherished view from your kitchen or living room, don't cover it up with a deck railing. If necessary, drop the deck down two or three steps or lower the deck far enough so that it does not need a railing.

Computer deck programs

Computer software programs are available to help plan your deck, but it often takes time to learn to run them. Many home centers and lumberyards offer computer deck programs and employees who know how to work them. Bring in a rough drawing with dimensions (height, width, and length) and ask for help.

Most programs produce several drawings—a plan view, an elevation, and a perspective view. They also give you a list of lumber and materials.

But these programs have limitations. A typical one gives only a couple of railing styles to choose from, and it cannot help plan an overhead structure or planter. It may not be able to handle an unusual or odd-shaped design. And it may not include structural requirements that differ from typical building codes. That's why even professional deck contractors find that it's quickest to draw plans by hand.

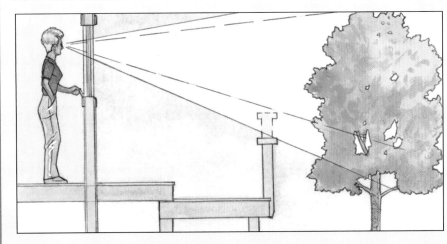

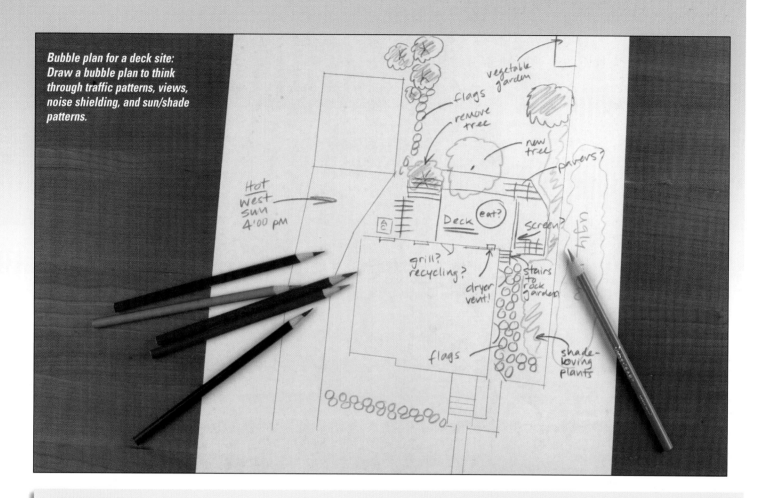

Bubble plan for a deck site: Draw a bubble plan to think through traffic patterns, views, noise shielding, and sun/shade patterns.

STANLEY PRO TIP: **Space requirements**

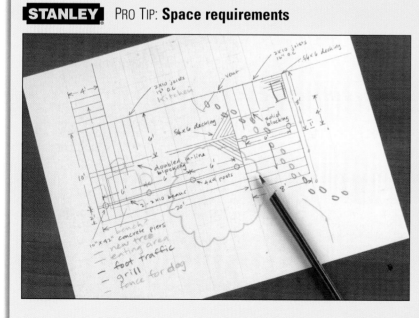

Many decks have plenty of square footage but feel cramped. That's because they were not planned with traffic and activity areas in mind. To avoid this problem, remember these general design rules:

■ **Pathways**—from the door to the stairs and between activity areas—must be 3½ to 4 feet wide at all points.

■ To accommodate a typical **round table** with six chairs, provide a circular area with a diameter of at least 9 feet.

■ A **rectangular table** should have an area 5 to 6 feet wider and longer than the table.

■ A simple **cooking area** with a grill and a small table usually needs an area about 6 feet square. Provide more room if there will be a counter or a large table.

■ For a single **reclining chair,** allow an area 4 feet by 7 feet. For two reclining chairs, allow 7 feet by 7 feet.

■ Locate the **stairway** so that it routes traffic around rather than through an activity area. Or expand a portion of the deck—a foot or so may make all the difference.

MAKING SURE IT'S STRONG

Five basic components make up any deck: decking, joists, beams (and possibly a ledger), posts, and footings. To ensure that a deck is strong enough to last for decades, local building departments have strict codes regarding the sizes and types of these components.

Lumber type
The strength of a board depends largely on two factors: its species and its quality. Among lumber commonly available in pressure-treated form for deck framing, Douglas fir is usually the best because it is strong and stable. Southern pine is just as strong, but it has more of a tendency to warp. "Hem-fir" is a vague designation encompassing several species of wood. Some hem-fir is fairly strong and stable, but other types are weak and tend to warp and crack. Consult with a lumber source and the building department before using hem-fir.

Lumber quality also has a bearing on a board's strength. Boards that are labeled "construction grade," "common," or "#3" generally have defects that may make them too weak for a deck structure. Boards labeled "#2 or better" are strong enough for most deck structures. "Select" or "#1" boards are virtually free of defects and are the strongest, but they are usually not worth the extra cost for use in deck building.

Footings
In areas with freezing winters, most codes require concrete footings that extend below the frostline. In warmer areas, a shallow footing is allowed, but codes will specify a minimum amount of mass in the footings. If an area has marshy or sandy soil, massive footings may be required.

Posts
For most decks, 4×4 lumber is strong enough for structural posts. If a deck is raised more than 6 feet above the ground, codes may require 6×6 posts.

Beams
The farther a beam must span—that is, the farther apart the posts are—the more massive a beam must be. The chart below lists approximate recommended spans. Beams made of two or more pieces are usually at least as strong as solid beams of the same size. For instance, a beam made of two 2×8s is probably stronger than a solid piece of 4×8. They are also less likely to crack.

Joists
The required width of a joist depends on its span—how far it must travel between beams or between a beam and a ledger. It also depends on the joist spacing; for instance, joists that are placed 24 inches apart must be wider than joists placed 16 inches apart. See the chart below and study your local code.

Decking
Decking boards span from joist to joist. If you use ¾ decking, joists must be no farther apart than 16 inches. Decking made of 2×4 or 2×6 can span up to 24 inches. If you will run decking at an angle, you may need to put the joists closer together; know your local codes.

Recommended beam spans

Beam spans	Beam	Joists span up to	Beam span
Distance between posts, using #2 or better Southern pine or Douglas fir	4×6	6'	6'
	4×8	6'	8'
	4×8	8'	7'
	4×8	11'	6'
	4×10	6'	10'
	4×10	8'	9'
	4×10	10'	8'
	4×10	12'	7'

Recommended joist spans

Beam spans	Joist	If joists are spaced	Span
Distance a joist spans between beams or between a beam and a ledger, using #2 or better Southern pine or Douglas fir	2×6	16"	9½'
	2×6	24"	8'
	2×8	16"	13'
	2×8	24"	10½'
	2×10	16"	16½'
	2×10	24"	13½'

Local codes

Your local building department has regulations designed to ensure a strong and durable deck. While a few requirements may seem dated or unusual, most are based on the following common concerns:

■ **Span** requirements (left) ensure your deck won't sag or collapse during a party or under snow load. Codes specify maximum spans according to the type of wood used.

■ A deck more than about 2 feet or two steps above ground must have a **railing.** Codes dictate how high the railing must be, as well as how far apart the balusters can be. Small children must not be able to climb it.

Some codes require hand rails, not just cap rails, for stairs.

■ If you attach the deck to the house with a **ledger,** code states how many fasteners of what type must be used. Metal flashing of a specific type may be required.

■ Many codes demand that posts be held in place by a specific type of **post anchor.**

■ In cold areas, many codes require **footings** that extend below the frostline, so that the deck does not get raised up in the winter by "frost heave." Other departments may allow for a "floating" deck with shallower footings that rise and fall together during freeze and thaw cycles.

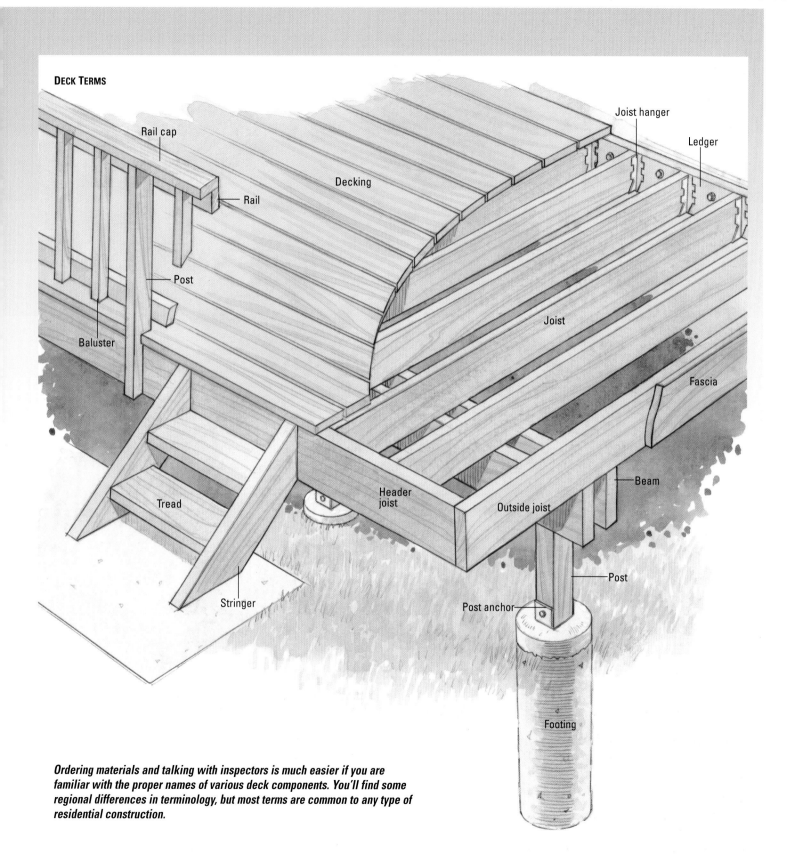

DECK TERMS

Rail cap

Decking

Joist hanger

Ledger

Rail

Post

Baluster

Joist

Fascia

Tread

Header joist

Stringer

Outside joist

Beam

Post

Post anchor

Footing

Ordering materials and talking with inspectors is much easier if you are familiar with the proper names of various deck components. You'll find some regional differences in terminology, but most terms are common to any type of residential construction.

BUILDING AN ABOVE-AVERAGE DECK

Compliance with building codes ensures that your deck will be solid and long-lasting. However, you may want to go beyond basics and add features to enhance the strength and beauty of your deck. Here are some suggestions.

Better-than-average materials

Though it will increase the cost, consider buying top-quality lumber for the visible parts of the deck. Redwood costs a lot more than pressure-treated, but it has a classic look that nothing else can match.

No matter which lumber you choose, carefully select boards for the most visible parts of the deck, such as the cap of the railing. "Select" or #1 grade lumber or lumber with a low moisture content will look good years later; #2 lumber may not.

Wherever fasteners will be visible, think carefully about how they will look. Stainless-steel screws or nails may seem like an extravagance, but they're worth it if you really like the way they look.

Planning visible joints

Wood joints on outdoor structures tend to separate over the years. Plan a deck with as few joints as possible and take a little extra time to make all the joints stronger.

Avoid fancy joinery unless you are an experienced carpenter using stable lumber. Setting boards into notches, for instance, may look good when first installed, but once the wood shrinks, the result will look sloppy. Avoid miter joints whenever possible; butt joints are easier to construct and less prone to separating.

Sometimes you can avoid butt joints in the decking if you buy extra-long boards. Eighteen- or 20-foot-long boards may cost more and be hard to find, but they're worth it if they eliminate joints.

Whenever there is the slightest chance that a nail or screw may split the board, drill a pilot hole before driving the fastener.

For the tightest joints, rent or buy a power miter saw *(pages 13, 29)*, which makes more accurate cuts than a circular saw.

If butt joints are necessary in the decking, attach a 2×4 cleat on the side of the joist to provide twice the nailing surface. Drill pilot holes before driving screws or nails through the decking boards. Consider installing a divider strip *(page 70)*.

The outside corner of a railing top cap is a notorious trouble spot. Wood biscuits reinforce this joint invisibly. While a biscuit joiner is expensive (you'll likely want to rent it), it is far easier, more forgiving, and stronger than dowels or other fasteners.

STANLEY PRO TIP: **2×4 decking with fewer fasteners**

Decking made of 2×4s rather than the standard 2×6 (or ⅝×6) makes a more complex decking pattern that many people find worth the extra cost and effort. If you use stable lumber with a low moisture content, only one nail or deck screw per joint is needed to hold the decking firmly in place. If using nails, be sure to buy galvanized spiral or ringshank nails. Screws should be galvanized or treated with nonstick coating.

Excavate the area and take steps to block weeds before building a deck, even if codes do not require these steps. This will help prevent mosquitoes from breeding in vegetation and keep unwanted shade-loving plants from growing up through the decking.

Cantilever the joists a few feet past the beam to hide some of the framing. If the underside is still visible, consider installing a skirt *(pages 104–105)*. Add an access door if you plan to store items under the deck.

This four-part rail post takes some time to build, but it has a more interesting appearance and is less likely to develop problems over the years than a single piece. Thick, wide boards are more likely to split than smaller boards. Even 4×4 posts often develop cracks.

Anchor stairway posts so they won't wobble from side to side. Most posts gain lateral strength by being attached to outside joists. However, the posts at the bottom of a stair rail are not connected to the deck and will be stronger if attached to a post anchor or sunk into a concrete footing *(page 75)*. Position the post back far enough so it has maximum contact with the stringer.

DRAWING A PLAN

You don't need fancy drafting tools to produce professional-looking plans for your deck. A pad of graph paper (use a ¼-inch grid), a pencil or two, a good eraser, and a ruler will do the job.

Check with your local building department to see whether it has specific requirements for plans. Start with rough drawings that show the basic contours of the deck. Then graduate to scale drawings. Create a final drawing that details board placement.

Satisfying the inspector

Your building department may have sample plans that you can use as guides for your own drawings. Most departments do not demand architect-quality plans, but they do want to see where all the pieces fit. Inspectors don't like to squint over unclear drawings, and they may want to see a complete list of all materials.

Produce at least one plan (overhead) view and one elevation (front and/or side) drawing. Include separate, enlarged detail drawings for all the parts that are complicated or unusual.

Use drawings to save time and money

Though it may seem tedious, draw every framing piece; this will show exactly how many boards of which sizes you need.

With a complete set of drawings in hand, you won't have to estimate materials; you can count the exact number of boards and hardware pieces you will need. Buy several extra pieces of each size, in case some turn out to be defective or are damaged.

Detailed drawings also can help you spot ways to save money on materials. For example, if a plan calls for joists that are 12 foot 2 inches long, you will need to buy 14-foot boards and waste nearly 2 feet of each piece. By shortening the deck a few inches, you can buy less expensive 12-foot joists.

Drawing careful plans enables you to solve problems before you start building—better to waste a little pencil lead than costly lumber and your valuable time. The more detailed and precise you make the drawings, the more likely you are to catch design flaws that would slow the building process. For example, draw in any outdoor receptacle boxes, faucets, or dryer vents that protrude from the side of the house; they may be in the way of where a ledger will be installed.

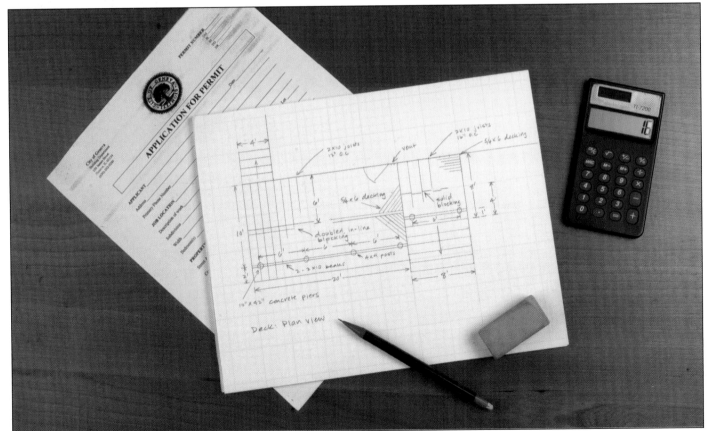

Draw a plan view from an overhead point of view. This important drawing must show all the joists, beams, posts, and stair framing. A plan view may also include a partial view of the decking, railing, and any other structures that are attached to the deck. Even though the drawing is to scale, be sure to include all dimensions, including overall length and width, how far apart the joists and beams are, and specific lengths of perimeter pieces. Show the locations and sizes of the house's windows and doors.

Include a materials list that states the number and size of all framing members as well as all hardware pieces.

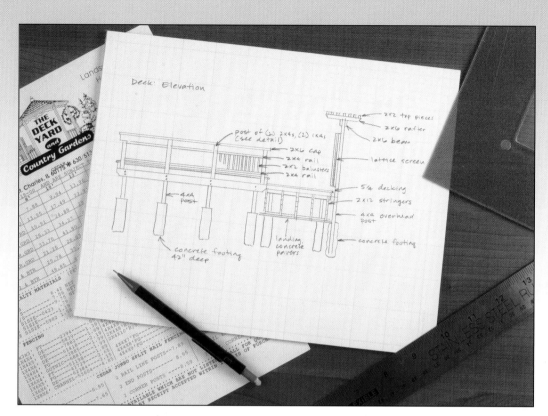

An elevation emphasizes vertical elements: footings, posts, railings, and any built-in planters, benches, or overhead structures. Produce one or two side views. Each elevation should show the size of the footings and the dimensions for the railing. Railing dimensions are particularly important. Indicate the height of the railing as well as how much space will be between balusters. Give the dimensions for all the railing pieces and describe how they will be attached.

Include information about fasteners. Indicate the size and number of screws or bolts used to attach the ledger, beams, and railing posts. If you will use special hardware, describe it in detail.

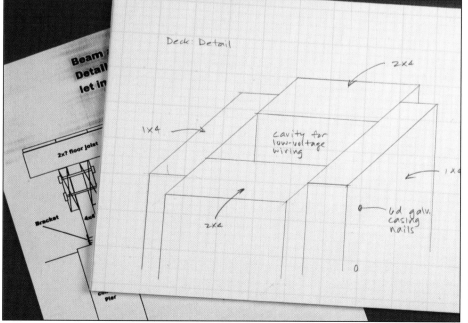

A separate detail drawing makes things clear if there is something that is too complicated to be shown on the plan view or elevation drawing. Use detail drawings to show framing for a change in deck levels, the method of attachment for a ledger, or an unusual stairway. Your building department may want detail drawings for the railing or for any permanent benches, planters, or overhead structures.

STANLEY PRO TIP

Dealing with inspectors

Building inspectors have an important job: They assure that all structures built in their area are strong and safe. To accomplish this goal, they are given the authority to stop construction on any job they feel is being built incorrectly. Work with an inspector in a respectful, businesslike manner. Present clean and complete drawings and materials lists. Find out how many inspections you will need and be ready for each. Do not cover up anything an inspector wants to look at, or you may have to dismantle your work. It's seldom a good idea to argue with an inspector. He or she knows more than you do, and getting on the bad side of an inspector can make a job miserable. Comply exactly with all of the inspector's directions.

BASIC SKILLS

If you're new to carpentry—or even if you're just a bit rusty—spend half a day or so practicing marking and cutting scrap boards. That way, a rookie mistake won't damage an expensive board.

Turning skills into habits

Precise measurements, straight cuts, and firm joints do not happen by accident. Learn the techniques that lead to professional results, then perform them over and over again until they become second nature.

It helps to have a predictable routine. Strap on a comfortable tool belt and keep basic tools—tape measure, pencil, knife, layout square—in assigned pockets. Jot down measurements rather than trying to memorize them. That way you can think about important things rather than looking for tools or trying to remember a number.

Keep tools in good shape

Keep a sharp blade in your saw and maintain a collection of sharp bits for the drill. If a measuring tool is damaged, replace it to ensure accuracy.

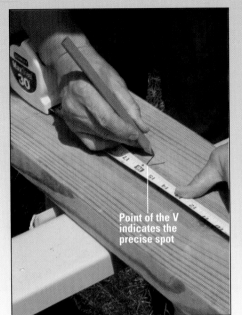

Point of the V indicates the precise spot

Layout square

Waste side mark

Before cutting a board, check the end that you won't cut, to make sure it is square. If not, cut it square and remeasure. Hook the tape measure to the board's end and extend the tape along the board. Mark the point of measurement with a V.

Hold the pencil tip on the point of the V, and slide a layout square over until it touches the pencil tip. Mark a straight line, then draw a large X to indicate the waste side of the cut.

STANLEY PRO TIP

Gloves or no gloves?

Gloves protect your hands from splinters and pressure-treatment. But wearing them makes it difficult to measure and mark precisely. Unless they fit tightly and are made of leather, gloves may cause a hammer to slip slightly out of your grasp. And loose-fitting gloves can be dangerous when using a circular saw. A solution: keep a pair of high-quality leather gloves in a pocket so you can put them on when handling heavy lumber and take them off when using tools.

Support the board so it won't bind and cause the saw to kick back dangerously as you cut. Support will also keep the board from splintering along the bottom edge as the waste piece falls away. If the waste side is less than 2 feet or so, support the board a little to the nonwaste side of the cutoff line so the waste portion can fall away when it is cut. If the waste side is longer, support the board in four places, as shown. That way, the board on both sides of the cut will stay still throughout the cut. As a bonus, this will make it easier for you to make a straight, neat cut.

Don't trust the bevel guide on a circular saw; it could be off by several degrees, producing nonsquare cuts. Use a layout square to check the blade angle and adjust the guide accordingly.

Begin the cut by positioning the saw blade to the waste side of the line, pulled back slightly from the board. Pull the trigger and push through the cut with a smooth stroke. Use a layout square. Avoid making slight turns as you cut. To cut thick lumber, mark around the piece and cut from two sides.

To make a rip cut (a cut along the length of a board), use the rip guide that comes with the circular saw. If the rip cut is not parallel to the edge of a board, either cut it freehand or clamp a long straightedge as a guide.

To make a 45-degree miter cut with a circular saw, clamp a layout square to the board as a guide. (Experiment to find the right distance away from the cut line.) Retract the blade guard before starting. Cut the miter before you cut the board to length so you can try again if you make a mistake.

Use a power miter saw, also called a chop saw, to make precise cuts easily. Make a long, stable work platform using sawhorses and 2× lumber. Screw the chop saw to the center of the platform. Add blocks of wood, the same height as the chop saw's base, on each side to support boards being cut.

SAFETY FIRST
Eye, ear, face protection

Cutting lumber, especially pressure-treated lumber, calls for protection. To protect eyes from flying chips and sawdust, wear safety glasses. If you are sensitive to pressure-treated lumber, use a face mask. When making frequent cuts with a circular saw or power miter saw, wear ear protection, in addition to other safety gear.

Basic skills (continued)

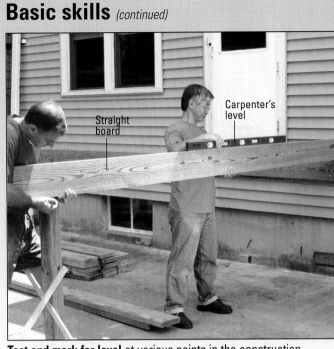

Test and mark for level at various points in the construction process. One way is to set a carpenter's level on top of a long, straight board. Position the level in the middle of the board's length, in case the board flexes slightly.

A water level makes it easy to check for level over a long distance and around corners. The simplest type involves two clear plastic tubes that attach to a garden hose. A valve on one tube lets you fill the hose with water. Run water through the hose to purge any air bubbles. Hold the tubes in place, wait a half minute for the water to stabilize, and check the water lines visible in the tubes for level.

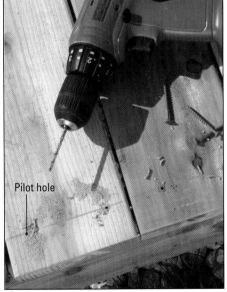

Drill a pilot hole whenever you will drive a nail or screw less than 2 inches from the edge of a board, to protect against splitting the board. Use a drill bit slightly thinner than the fastener and drill only through the board to be fastened, not the board beneath.

Equip the drill with a magnetic sleeve and a drill bit that matches the head of the screws you will drive. The magnetic feature allows you to work hands-free when driving short screws in awkward places.

Attach with angle-driven screws when you can only get at the end of the board to be fastened. Drill pilot holes at a steep angle and drive the screws until the heads start to bite into the board.

To start a nail, press the tip into the board and hold it with one hand while tapping with a hammer. Once the nail stands by itself, remove your hand and pound. Swing the hammer with a fluid motion and a flexible wrist, ending each stroke with a snap.

To set a nail, pound until the nailhead rests flush with the wood surface. Practice this until you can do it consistently without marring the surface of the wood. Use a nail set, which allows you to force the nailhead into the wood without marring the wood.

Attach with "toenails," fasteners driven at an angle, where necessary. Drill pilot holes at a steep angle and then drive the nail or screw. When using a nail, finish by using a nail set to pound the head slightly beneath the surface of the wood.

For extra-strong fastening, use lag screws or bolts. Temporarily support the board so it will not move as you work. Drill a pilot hole. Slide a washer onto the lag screw and tap it partway into the hole. Drive it home using a socket and ratchet wrench.

To attach with a carriage bolt, temporarily support the board so it will not move as you work. Drill a hole the same diameter as the bolt's shaft through both boards. Tap the bolt all the way through. Slip on a washer and tighten the nut.

Round the exposed edges with a hand sanding block before applying finish to a deck. (For this purpose, hand sanding is easier than power sanding.) To achieve uniform results, use long strokes whenever possible. Apply only moderate pressure.

FREESTANDING BASIC DECK

PLANTERS & BENCHES

This deck is made of two rectangles that overlap each other by 2 feet. Planters and benches help define two distinct areas. Because it sits low to the ground, no railing is required.

Footings and beams

The soil near the foundation of a new home—soil that was backfilled after the concrete basement was poured—is unstable. Local codes usually require that concrete footings within 3 feet of the foundation must be 8 feet deep. To avoid the time, effort, and expense of such deep footings, this plan makes use of heavy-duty beams that rest on footings placed farther away from the house. The beams, made of three 2×10s, run perpendicular to the house and are strong enough to cantilever 3 feet past the footings. The middle beam supports both deck levels.

Framing

The decking is pressure-treated ⅝×6 laid at a 45-degree angle to the house. For proper support, the joists must be spaced no more than 12 inches apart. If thicker 2× decking is used, or if the ¾ decking is run perpendicular to the joists, then the joists could be placed 16 inches apart (see the span chart on *page 22*).

Framing for the upper level rests on top of the lower-level framing and overlaps by 2 feet.

Using pressure-treated wood

Inexpensive pressure-treated lumber is used for the visible parts—the decking, benches, and planter—and the structural members. Many decks made of pressure-treated lumber lose their looks: The wood warps, splits, and turns an ugly gray. But with a little extra care, a treated-wood deck can look great for many years.

Choose boards that are straight, dry, and free of large knots *(page 16)*. Pressure-treated wood may twist and warp as it dries, so stack it tightly until you install it and fasten it securely. After a month or so, check to see whether any fasteners are working loose. If so, remove them and install longer fasteners.

This basic deck makes use of low-cost materials and simple construction techniques.

CHAPTER PREVIEW

Laying out the deck
page 34

Forming footings
page 38

Installing posts
page 42

Framing
page 44

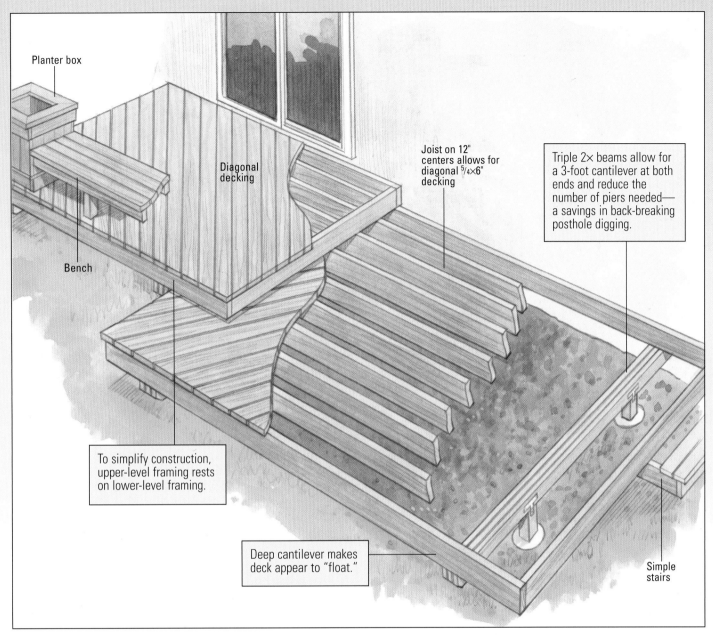

Planter box

Bench

Diagonal decking

Joist on 12" centers allows for diagonal ⁵/₄×6" decking

Triple 2× beams allow for a 3-foot cantilever at both ends and reduce the number of piers needed— a savings in back-breaking posthole digging.

To simplify construction, upper-level framing rests on lower-level framing.

Deep cantilever makes deck appear to "float."

Simple stairs

A two-level deck smoothes the transition from doorstep to yard, while adding enough visual interest to make even a small deck a desirable addition to a home. This deck uses pressure-treated lumber exclusively.

Angled decking
page 50

Simple stairs
page 53

Bench with planters
page 54

LAYING OUT THE DECK

The simple design of this deck includes fail-safe features—for instance, the beams may be off by an inch or so without weakening the structure. Don't take the project lightly, however. Produce an accurate scale drawing and get it approved by your building department *(pages 26–27)*. Keep in mind that the decking will overhang the joists by 1½ inches or so on all sides. If the yard is heavily sloped, see *pages 62–63* for tips.

Planning the footings and beams

Because they will extend 3 feet beyond the footings, massive beams made of three 2×10s are required. Large beams call for larger-than-average supports—4×6 posts and 12-inch-diameter footings.

PRESTART CHECKLIST

☐ **TIME**
Four to five hours to build batterboards, figure the layout, stretch lines, and determine footing locations

☐ **TOOLS**
Drill, sledgehammer, tape measure, mason's line, carpenter's square, shovel

☐ **SKILLS**
Measuring and checking for square, fastening with screws, pounding stakes

☐ **PREP**
Get drawings approved and double-check them for accuracy. Make sure you understand how every aspect of the deck will be assembled.

☐ **MATERIALS**
1×4 or 1×2 for stakes, 1⅝-inch screws, masking tape

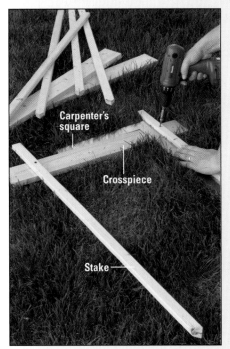

Carpenter's square
Crosspiece
Stake

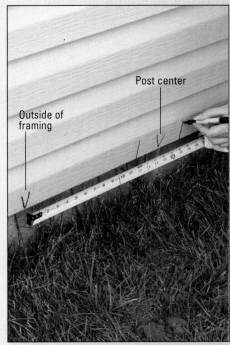

Outside of framing
Post center

1 Construct batterboards using 1×2s and 1×4s. Stakes can be from 16 to 36 inches long. If the ground is hard, make them shorter; if soft, make them longer. Cut the crosspieces about 30 inches long. Assemble the pieces with a single screw at each joint.

2 Mark the house wall for the positions of the posts. First, mark the outside of the framing (the decking will overhang it by 1½ inches). Then measure over and mark where the post will be located. Make sure you identify the center of the post.

LOCATING PIERS

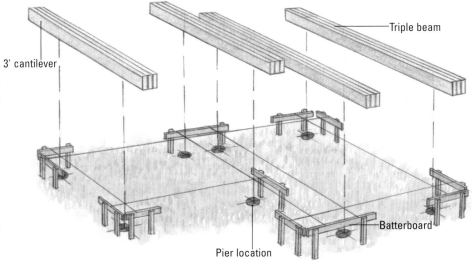

3' cantilever
Triple beam
Batterboard
Pier location

Batterboards support strings that help pinpoint the center of each post and pier. In this case, the piers are positioned 3 feet from the house to avoid the backfill next to the foundation of this new house.

3 Near the house, drive a batterboard into the ground, more or less centered over the post location. Pound the stakes until the crosspiece is 6 inches or so above the ground and stable. For soft, wet soil, use long stakes; shorter stakes are fine for hard ground.

4 Measure out from the house for the position of a post and drive in another batterboard. Position all batterboards about 2 feet beyond the post locations. To keep your estimated post locations roughly perpendicular to the house, hold a carpenter's square against the house and run a tape measure along its side, as shown.

STANLEY PRO TIP: **Build the frame first**

If your deck has a simple design and the yard is level, here's a reliable method of laying out the footing locations. Assemble the outside joists *(page 47)* and lay them on the ground exactly below where they will go. Check that the corners are square *(page 37)* and drive stakes to hold the boards firmly in place. You now have a perfect indicator of the framing. String lines and measure from the house to mark for the post locations.

Laying out the deck *(continued)*

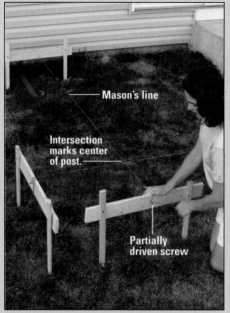

5 Estimate the location of the other postholes. Drive additional batterboards into the ground, about 2 feet beyond the post locations.

6 Drive a screw partway into the middle of each batterboard's cross piece. Stretch mason's line to form a grid. Use the screws to anchor the string. String lines should intersect at roughly the same height. Drive one of the batterboards deeper into the ground, if necessary, to align the strings.

7 Adjust the string that runs parallel to the house until it is the correct distance from the house, where the center of the posts will be, and parallel to the house. Anchor this string firmly to its batterboards so that it cannot be bumped out of position.

Laying out with boards

If the deck is small, you can lay out a deck using straight boards instead of batterboards and string lines. Position the boards so their inside edges are in the same locations as the string lines would be (see Step 6). Use the 3–4–5 method (Step 8, *page 37)* to check that the boards are square to each other and to the house. Measure along the boards and mark the ground for the post locations. You'll need to reassemble this layout structure when it comes time to insert the J-bolts into the concrete (Step 7, *page 40).*

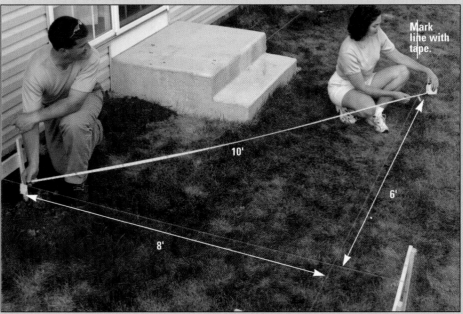

8 Check the string lines for square. Measure 6 feet along one line and mark the spot with a piece of tape. Measure 8 feet along the perpendicular string line and mark it the same way. (Make sure you know which side of the tape indicates the exact spot.) Measure the distance between the two marks; if it is exactly 10 feet then the lines are square to each other. If not, adjust one string line. With this method, you can substitute 6, 8, and 10 with any multiples of 3, 4, and 5; for example 9, 12, and 15; or 12, 16, and 20. The larger the numbers, the greater the accuracy.

9 Once you have found the correct position for the string, mark its position on a batterboard with a pencil. Remove the screw and drive it into the correct spot. Wrap the string tightly around the crosspiece and tie it to the screw.

Keep it stable

Layout problems often arise not because of inaccurate measurements but because things get bumped. So pound batterboards in until they're firm. Clearly mark the correct spot for the string on each batterboard. Keep neighborhood kids away from batterboards and string lines. When walking around the job site, step carefully around or over the string lines. Most importantly, check and double-check measurements to be sure things are square. Check measurements:
- When you start to dig the holes
- When you insert the tube forms
- When you insert the J-bolts

Locating posts precisely

To mark the center of a posthole, hold a plumb bob (a chalk line works fine) with its string barely touching each layout line. Drive a stake into the ground to mark the spot.

If the design calls for three or more posts supporting the same beam, the middle posts do not require intersecting string lines. Just measure along the string line and mark with a stake.

FORMING FOOTINGS

Check with a building inspector for advice on how to excavate your site and prevent the growth of weeds. In some locations, there is no need to excavate—building the deck will kill all foliage under the deck. In many areas, however, you must remove all sod, lay down thick plastic or weed block, and cover it with gravel to keep things from growing.

Local codes have requirements for posthole depth and width, as well as specifications for how the concrete should be formed and how the post will attach to the concrete. These steps show the most common method, using a tube form and a post anchor that attaches with a J-bolt.

Digging in

Digging is back-straining work, especially if you are not used to doing it. Don't rush it. When possible, work with your back straight, rather than bent. Consider renting a power auger (below right) and hiring some help. Or call fencing or landscaping contractors and ask how much they would charge to dig the holes.

PRESTART CHECKLIST

☐ **TIME**
To dig a posthole, from 15 minutes to 2 hours, depending on soil conditions

☐ **TOOLS**
Posthole digger or power auger, spade, level, layout square, trowel

☐ **SKILLS**
Using a spade or a posthole digger

☐ **PREP**
Have utility companies mark locations of water, gas, electric, or phone lines. Double-check that the locations for the postholes are correct.

☐ **MATERIALS**
Sand or flour for marking the ground, plastic sheeting, gravel, concrete, tube forms, J-bolts

1 Remove the string lines, but keep the batterboards in place. Take care not to disturb the batterboards as you work. Use string lines, sand, or spray paint to mark the area that will be covered by the deck. Dig away the sod from the deck area.

2 It may be possible to slice lines in the ground with a straight-bladed spade and roll up the sod for use elsewhere. Leave the stakes that mark the post locations in place, or pick them up and replace them as soon as you have rolled up the sod around them.

Post location — Sod

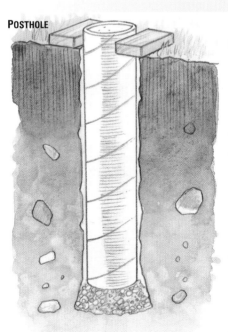

POSTHOLE

Shovel a few inches of gravel into the hole to provide drainage at the bottom of the post. Use a piece of 4×4 to tamp the gravel firm.

Rent a power auger

Handle bars
Shock bar
Auger
Hydraulic power source

A rented power auger speeds up the digging and makes holes that are more precise than those dug by hand. A handheld auger may be difficult to use, especially if the soil is rocky or full of roots. This type has a bar that helps absorb the shock when the tool bucks as it hits a root or rock.

3 For each posthole, remove the stake and make a large X mark on the ground with flour, sand, or spray paint. Dig a hole wide enough to accommodate the tube form that you will use. Shovel a few inches of gravel into the hole and tamp it down.

4 Place a length of concrete tube form into the hole and mark it for cutting about 2 inches above grade. Cut the form with a handsaw or a knife. Check that the top of the form is close to level; recut the form if necessary. Anchor the form with screws driven into 2×s laid flat on the ground.

5 Don't fill the tubes with concrete until the inspector has signed off on the holes. Fill any spaces around the form with well-packed soil. Mix the concrete and pour it into the form. Poke a pole or a piece of 1×2 into the concrete several times to remove any air bubbles.

WHAT IF…
You need lots of concrete?

If you have a lot of concrete to pour, using dry-mix bags will be time-consuming and expensive. Explore some other options:

■ Most ready-mix concrete companies deliver only large loads, but some have special trucks made for small jobs. The company can help you figure out how much concrete you need. Plan how to move the concrete from the truck to the holes—having a couple of helpers and wheelbarrows is a good idea, since the drivers will not wait around for a long time.

■ Consider renting a gas- or electric-powered concrete mixer. Pour bags of dry-mix into the mixer and add water, or have cement, sand, and gravel delivered to your yard and mix your own. A common ratio is one part cement, one part sand, and two parts gravel.

Mixing concrete

A 60-pound bag of dry-mix will fill about 20 inches of an 8-inch tube form, or 13 inches of a 10-inch form, or 9 inches of a 12-inch form. If you need more than 40 bags, consider having concrete delivered (see box at left). To mix concrete, pour a bag of dry-mix into a wheelbarrow or tub and dig out a small hole in the middle. Pour or spray water into the

hole, taking care not to add too much.

Mix with a shovel or a hoe. Scrape the wheelbarrow or tub as you mix so there is no dry powder left at the bottom.

A good mix is just loose enough to be pourable but not too runny. It should hold its shape and cling for at least 1 second to a shovel held vertically.

Forming footings (continued)

6 Drag a short board across the top of the form, using a sawing motion. This removes excess concrete and partially smooths the concrete surface.

7 Reattach the string lines and check that they are square *(pages 36–37).* Directly below intersecting lines, insert a J-bolt into the concrete. Wiggle it downward until about 1 inch sticks up.

8 Use a layout square to check that the bolt is pointing straight up. With a trowel, smooth the concrete. Check the bolt again.

STANLEY PRO TIP: **"Quick-set" piers**

In areas where the ground does not freeze in winter, deep footings may not be required. However, the footings must be large enough to support heavy weight. Wide, shallow footings may be required.

Not all areas with winter freezing need deep footings. Decks on shallow footings will "float"—rise and fall an inch or so with the freezing and thawing of the soil. Check local codes.

If the ground is stable and you don't mind using more concrete, you can skip the tube form and pour directly into a hole in the ground. However, there should be a form at the top of the footing so that the footing protrudes a couple of inches above ground level.

A 2×4 frame set atop a wide, shallow hole is a simple way to form a footing. Check that the frame is level.

A precast pier can be set into a bed of concrete while it is still wet. If the soil is firm, local codes may allow a series of precast piers set directly on the ground.

9 Once the concrete has set, smooth the landscaped area and tamp it firm by walking on it. Fill any indentations that would create puddles. Make sure that the footings stick up at least 2 inches above the ground. Spread heavy-duty plastic sheeting or weed block over the deck area to prevent the growth of weeds. Use gravel or stones—not soil—to hold the plastic in place. If you need two or more sheets, overlap them at least 1 foot.

10 Pour 1 or 2 inches of gravel on top of the plastic and rake it smooth. The gravel will poke small holes in the plastic, which will allow water to seep through. However, avoid large holes or tears that may permit the growth of weeds.

Groundcover options

For long-lasting insurance against the growth of weeds, lay down black plastic sheeting that's 6 mils thick. Landscaping fabric protects against weeds but does not last as long as plastic. Purchase staplelike stakes to hold the sheeting in position.

You'll be walking on top of the gravel while you build the framing, so choose gravel that is free of sharp edges, which could tear the plastic. Pea gravel or lava stone are two good choices.

Weed block

Heavy-gauge plastic

Pea gravel

Lava stone

River rock

WHAT IF...
Drainage is a concern?

If rain and melting snow threaten to cascade off the edges of the deck and erode planting areas, the simplest solution is to dig a trench around the deck—6 inches deep or so—and fill it with gravel. This catches runoff from the deck and lets it seep into the ground. If drainage problems threaten your foundation or crawlspace, you may need to dig a long drainage trench that slopes away from the deck. Lay perforated drainpipe in the trench and have the pipe end in a dry well—a gravel-filled hole in the ground that is at least 1 foot in diameter and 2 feet deep.

INSTALLING POSTS

Allow a day or two for the concrete to set and start to cure; it will take a week or so to achieve full strength.

A post level is an indispensible tool for installing posts. It quickly tells you whether the post is plumb in both directions at once and leaves both hands free to work.

High-quality pressure-treated posts are fully saturated with a chemical that will keep them from rotting for decades. For an extra measure of protection, soak the cut ends in a bucket of sealer before installing them *(page 17)*.

Use a level and a long board to estimate the height of each post. Cut posts that are about a foot too long; you will cut them to exact height later.

These steps show how to cut posts that will have beams placed on top of them. For a sandwiched beam, see *page 44*.

PRESTART CHECKLIST

☐ **TIME**
About 30 minutes to install a post anchor, temporarily brace a post, measure and cut a post to height

☐ **TOOLS**
Post level, hammer, drill, tape measure, circular saw, layout square, wrench

☐ **SKILLS**
Driving screws, checking for level and plumb, cutting with a circular saw

☐ **PREP**
Pour footings with J-bolts. Use string lines to mark the footings for posts that are correctly aligned *(page 34–37)*.

☐ **MATERIALS**
Posts (usually 4×4s), adjustable post anchors, 1×4s or 1×2s for braces and stakes, 2-inch screws

Post level

Post anchor

1 Install a post anchor and finger-tighten the hold-down nut so that the anchor is fairly stable but movable. Insert a post and attach a post level to it. Drive stakes and attach braces to them with screws. Position the post so it is plumb and screw the braces to the post.

Top of decking at this height

2 Use a level to mark the first post for the height of the decking. Make sure that the decking will be at least 1 inch below the threshold of the doorway.

WHAT IF...
You have to add a bolt after the concrete has set?

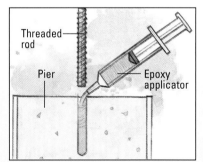

Threaded rod

Pier

Epoxy applicator

If you forgot to install a J-bolt or if one is misaligned, buy threaded rods and epoxy made for retrofitting concrete anchors. Drill a hole in the footing using a masonry bit slightly larger in diameter than the rod. Vacuum out all the dust. Squirt epoxy into the hole and insert the threaded rod. The epoxy will set firm in about a day.

STANLEY PRO TIP

Installing post anchors

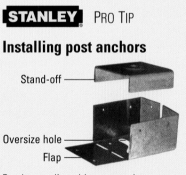

Stand-off

Oversize hole

Flap

Purchase adjustable post anchors, so you can move them over ½ inch to correct small mistakes. Choose those with a "stand-off" that holds the post away from moisture.

Install the anchor with one flap down and finger-tighten the hold-down nut. Install the posts and drive nails or screws to secure the posts. Use string lines to check that the posts are lined up correctly. When you are sure it's right, tighten the nuts, using an open-end or crescent wrench. Lift the flap and attach it to the post.

Top of decking
Top of joist
Top of beam

Cutline for post

3 Measure down from the top of the decking. Strike marks to indicate the thickness of the decking, the depth of the joists, and the depth of the beam. Use a circular saw to cut the post to this height.

4 You can use a line level or a water level to mark all of the posts for cutting level to the first post. Or you can use a straight board and a carpenter's level, as shown. Set one end of the board on the first post. If you are holding the board against more than one post, it might help to have someone hold the other end of the board. Mark all the posts and double-check that the marks are all level with each other; then cut the posts.

Options for Setting Posts

Some deck designs call for posts that are set in holes filled with concrete or tamped dirt. The concrete method is challenging because all the posts must be perfectly aligned when the concrete is poured.

A 42-inch-deep hole is typical for both methods. Tamp the bottom of the hole and throw in a few inches of gravel. Tamp the gravel. Insert the post.

If you will be filling around the post with concrete, brace the post plumb in both directions. Drive several 16d nails into the post to help anchor it in the concrete.

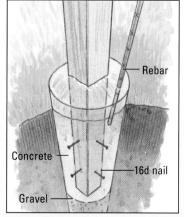

Rebar

Concrete

16d nail

Gravel

As you fill around a post with concrete, poke down with a piece of metal reinforcing rod or a 1×2 to eliminate air pockets. Mound the concrete around the post above the hole to drain water.

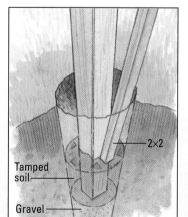

2×2

Tamped soil

Gravel

When setting a post in soil, tamp down every few inches of soil. Check frequently that the post remains plumb in both directions as you tamp and fill.

STANLEY PRO TIP

J-bolt too long?

If a J-bolt is too tall to accommodate the post anchor (a common mistake), add a few washers before screwing down the nut. Or trim the bolt with a hacksaw. Before you cut, spin on a nut to below the cut line. After cutting, remove the nut to clean and realign the threads.

FRAMING

The beam for this deck is extra heavy-duty, made of three 2×10s. (For more standard methods of beam construction, see *page 65*.)

Many older decks were built using massive timbers—4×6s or 4×8s, for example—for beams. Some builders still do it that way; using a one-piece beam can save time. But large timbers are heavy. They often warp beyond remedy, and they almost surely will develop cracks over the years. Fastening two pieces of 2× lumber together actually creates a beam that is stronger than a single piece of 4× lumber.

If a deck design is complicated, it often makes sense to build a beam that is about 1 foot too long and cut it to length after the framing is in place *(page 68)*. This deck is simple enough that the beams can be cut to exact length before they are installed.

PRESTART CHECKLIST

☐ **TIME**
About 2 hours to build a 14-foot-long beam made of three 2×10s with plywood spacers

☐ **TOOLS**
Tape measure, circular saw, drill, long bit, hammer, clamps, adjustable or socket wrench

☐ **SKILLS**
Measuring and cutting a board, fastening with screws and bolts

☐ **PREP**
Set up two or three stable sawhorses and lay the beam pieces on them

☐ **MATERIALS**
Lumber for the beam pieces (2×10s in this case), pressure-treated plywood, 1¼-inch deck screws, 3-inch deck screws, ⅜-inch × 6-inch carriage bolts with nuts and washers

A. Making a beam

Decorative angle

Plywood spacer

1 Cut the three beam pieces to length. Lay them on top of each other with their crowns *(page 17)* facing the same direction and check that they are all the same length. If you choose to do so, cut a decorative angle at one or both ends.

2 From a sheet of ½-inch pressure-treated plywood, cut pointed spacers. (The points prevent rainwater from sitting on the plywood and soaking in.) Use 1¼-inch screws to attach a spacer, pointing at the crown-up side, every 16 inches or so to two beam pieces.

OVERVIEW OF BEAM LOCATION

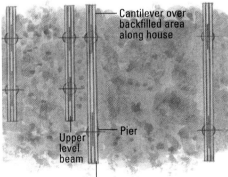

Cantilever over backfilled area along house

Pier

Upper level beam

Lower level beam

Be sure to assemble the beam so the 2×s have the crown sides up. Plywood spacers point upward.

Sandwiching the post

Sandwiching post between two 2×s is the simplest and most common beam approach. Begin by cutting your posts about 1 foot longer than needed. Set them in place with temporary support. Position the members and fasten them with carriage bolts (see *pages 88–90*).

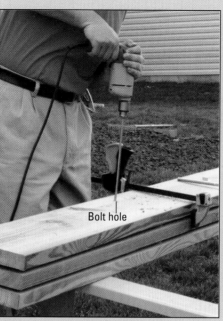

3 Stack two beam pieces with the spacers sandwiched between. Check that they are aligned at the ends and clamp together. Nail 16d galvanized box nails or drive 3-inch screws every 16 inches alternating the distance from the edge of the beam. Add the third beam piece and repeat the process.

4 Using a long drill bit of the same diameter as the bolts, drill two holes through the beam every 16 inches. The holes should be about 2 inches from the top and bottom edges of the boards.

5 Tap carriage bolts through the holes. On the flip side, add a washer and nut and tighten, using a crescent or socket wrench *(page 31)*.

WHAT IF...
The deck is close to the ground?

If a deck is low to the ground, there may not be enough vertical room for the joists to rest on top of a beam. The solution is a flush beam, which is essentially a header that has been doubled for strength. Cut two headers (the boards that will be perpendicular to the joists) and draw layout lines on them indicating where the joists will go (Step 3, *page 47)*. Fasten them to the posts so they are level. Double up the headers to make them flush beams. Drive a pair of nails or screws every 16 inches or so to bind the pieces together firmly. The second piece is 3 inches longer than the header joist to accommodate an outside joist on both sides of the frame.

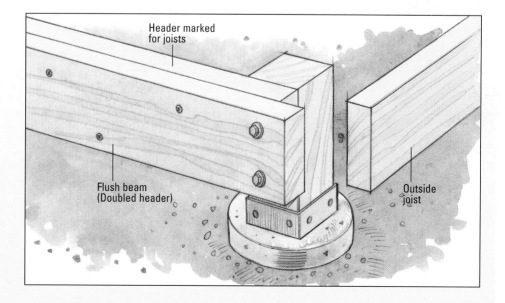

B. Beams, headers, and outside joists

1 Mark the beam where it will overhang the posts on both ends. In this case the beam is marked 3 feet from each end. Then have someone help you place the beam on top of the posts. For the longer beams you may need two helpers. Make sure that the beams are flush to the posts on both sides.

2 Confirm that the beam is level. If it isn't, trim one of the posts. If that will lower the deck too much, cut a new post; do not shim up the beam to make it level. Attach the beam to the post with T-brackets and joist-hanger screws or nails on both sides of each beam.

T-bracket

FRAMING OVERVIEW

Outside joist

Blocking

Header joist

Header joist

Joist

Header joist, upper level

A framing plan shows the exact location of every joist. Pay attention to details, such as the exact length of the headers.

Outside joist

Header joist

Outside joist

Joist goes on this side of the line.

3 Cut the two header joists to length. Use the straightest boards possible. Lay them on a flat surface, side by side, with crowns facing in opposite directions. See that the ends are perfectly aligned at both sides. Mark the headers with the joist locations indicated on the framing plan, 12 inches apart in this example. Every 12 inches, make a small V-shaped mark. Draw square lines through the marks, as shown. Draw an X on the joist side of the line.

Header joist

Outside joist

4 Cut the outside joists to length—usually the width of the framing minus 3 inches for the thickness of the two headers. On a flat surface, assemble the outside joists and the headers. Make sure the headers face each other correctly with their crowns up and the Xs on the same sides of the layout lines. Use a framing square to check that the frame is at least close to square. Drill pilot holes and drive nails or screws to attach the boards at the corners.

5 Check again for square, using the 3–4–5 method *(page 37)*. Attach a temporary brace at each corner to keep the frame stable when you lift it up. For the brace, use a 1×4 or larger, and attach it with two screws at each joint.

6 With a helper or two, lift the frame and set it on top of the beams. Measure the frame at all four points to make sure it overhangs the beams correctly. Check again for square using the 3–4–5 method. Attach the frame to the beam with a hurricane tie *(page 19)* or similar piece of hardware at each joint.

C. Inside joists

Pattern joist

Temporary cleat

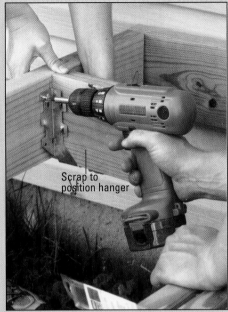

Scrap to position hanger

1 In this design, the inside joists are the same length as the outside joists. Cut the inside joists using factory methods. Set up a cutting platform so you can move boards on and off easily and work comfortably. Make sure the boards will be properly supported while you cut (*page 28*). Check the ends; if one is not square or has a split, cut off 1 or 2 inches. Use one joist as a pattern, attaching a temporary cleat to one end. Measure and mark for the cut; draw an X to indicate which side of the line will be cut. Cut with a power miter box, a radial arm saw, or a circular saw.

2 Install the joist hangers on the outside joists. Line up one side of the hanger on the vertical mark on the header so that the hanger overlaps the X. Fasten one side in place, then have a helper hold a scrap of joist so you can position and fasten the other side of the hanger.

WHAT IF...
The deck wraps around a corner?

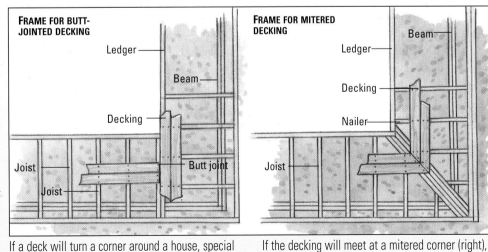

FRAME FOR BUTT-JOINTED DECKING

Ledger

Beam

Decking

Joist

Joist

Butt joint

FRAME FOR MITERED DECKING

Ledger

Beam

Decking

Nailer

Joist

If a deck will turn a corner around a house, special framing is needed. The decking pattern determines the framing configuration. If the deck boards will meet in a butt joint (left), the framing is simple.

If the decking will meet at a mitered corner (right), support the miter joint with two joists installed at a 45-degree angle; attach a 2×4 nailer to each side, for added nailing surface.

Nails or screws?

Some building departments insist on nails designed exclusively for joist hangers—and they want one placed in every hole in the hanger. Others want screws made for hangers and assert that too many fasteners can split the joist. Check your local requirements. In any case, use only fasteners that are specially hardened and strong enough for use with joists.

3 Attach the joists to the joist hangers. Temporarily screw a block to the top of the joist and use it to hang the end of the joist onto the header. Slide a joist hanger tight to the bottom of the joist. Drive joist hanger nails or screws into each hole.

4 Check that the outside joists are straight. String a line as shown. Check several points along the string to make sure that it is an equal distance from the end joists. Use the 3–4–5 method to confirm that the frame is square.

5 Blocking keeps joists from warping and stiffens the framing. Snap a chalk line down the center of the joist run. Using the same stock as used for the joists, cut pieces 1½ inches shorter than the joist spacing and install them in a staggered pattern that allows you to face-nail each one.

STANLEY PRO TIP: **Attaching joists to the beam**

For extra stability, fasten the joists to the beam. Local codes may recommend simply toe-nailing or toe-screwing: Drill a pilot hole, then drive a 16d nail or 3-inch screw at a fairly steep angle through the joist and into the beam.

Or you may be required to use special hardware, such as hurricane or seismic ties. Slip one into place and drive four nails or screws to fasten it.

WHAT IF...
Joist hangers aren't required?

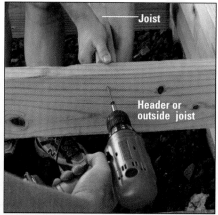

Local codes may allow you to back-nail (or back-screw) instead of attaching with joist hangers. Have a helper hold the joist in position while you drive 16d galvanized nails or 3-inch deck screws through the header and into the joist.

ANGLED DECKING

Installing decking at a 45-degree angle is not difficult if you start with the correct angle and follow layout plans. Practice to make sure you can consistently cut decking boards at a precise 45-degree angle. Measure carefully to see that the first boards are installed correctly. The rest of the boards will go on quickly.

Cutting the angles

A radial-arm saw or a 12-inch power miter saw is ideal for cutting 2×6 or 5⁄4 decking. With a 10-inch power miter box you may have to finish each cut with a handsaw— a time-consuming extra step. With practice, you can make accurate 45-degree cuts with a circular saw, using a layout square or a jig as a guide *(page 95)*. Some circular saws manage this more easily than others; often, the blade guard gets in the way at the beginning of the cut.

PRESTART CHECKLIST

☐ **TIME**
Most of a day to cut and install angled decking on a 300-square-foot deck

☐ **TOOLS**
Power miter saw or radial-arm saw, circular saw, tape measure, chalk line, flat pry bar, chisel, hammer, drill, hand saw, layout square

☐ **SKILLS**
Making accurate 45-degree cuts, driving screws or nails, cutting with a circular saw

☐ **PREP**
Check that the framing is securely fastened at all points

☐ **MATERIALS**
Decking, screws or nails

¼" plywood strip

1 To help maintain a straight line near the house, temporarily attach a strip of ¼-inch plywood against the siding, resting on top of the ledger. Make sure it can be removed after the decking is installed.

2 Choose two straight boards and cut one end of each at a 45-degree angle. A 10-inch power miter saw will not cut all the way across the board. Complete the cut with a handsaw. Or, if you are experienced using a power miter saw, lift up on the forward edge of the board to finish the cut.

STANLEY PRO TIP: **Buy the right lengths**

If possible, buy decking boards long enough so you will not need to make any butt joints. Make a scale drawing that shows every piece of decking, and measure to find out how many boards of each size you will need. The minimum length you can buy usually is 8 feet. If you need two 4-foot pieces, buy an 8-footer; if you need two 6-foot pieces, buy a 12-footer.

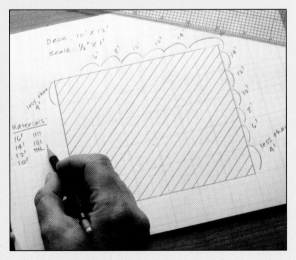

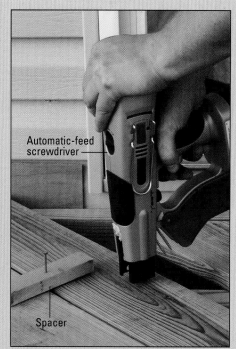

Automatic-feed screwdriver

Measurements should be equal

Spacer

3 Set the two boards on the framing with the miter-cut ends pressed against the spacer strip. Measure from the corner to the decking in both directions. When the two measurements are the same, the decking is at a 45-degree angle to the house.

Check the first board for straightness and fasten it to the joists with nails or screws. You may choose to drive all the fasteners as you go, or to drive only a few at this point and use chalk lines to line up all the other fasteners *(page 72)*.

4 Attach deck boards by driving two nails or screws wherever a board rests on a joist. Insert nails between the boards to maintain even spacing. An automatic-feed screwdriver (shown above) makes the job go quickly. Set the nail or screw heads slightly below the face of the decking.

Bending a warped board

Chisel

1 If a decking board is bowed, you will need to bend it into place. Insert spacers and fasten one end of the board. Then move along the board, straightening it as you go. Where a board needs persuading, drive a fastener partway into the board, push it into position, and finish driving the fastener.

2 If pushing does not do the trick, dig the point of a chisel or pry bar into the joist, right up against the decking board, and pry the board into position. If a board is so badly bowed that neither of these techniques works, return it to the lumberyard.

Easy spacers

Traditionally decking boards are spaced apart from each other using 16d nails. (Don't try using screws as spacers; they're hard to pull out.) If you drill a pilot hole and drive nails through small scrap blocks of wood, as shown, you'll have spacers that are easy to insert and remove. Make about a dozen spacers.

Angled decking (continued)

5 To mark the decking for a 1½-inch overhang, hold a piece of 2× lumber (which is actually 1½ inches thick) under the decking and use it as a gauge to mark both ends of the cut.

6 Give your chalk line box a good shake to make sure the line is well loaded with chalk. Hook the line onto a nail or screw driven partway into the side of one of the marked boards. Be sure to pull straight up when you snap the chalk line.

7 With clamps or deck screws, temporarily attach a straight board to the decking to serve as a guide for cutting along the chalk line. Cut the line with a circular saw.

STANLEY PRO TIP: **Doing it right**

Decking can be tedious work, but maintain your focus to achieve a deck surface with consistent joints and straight boards. Follow these tips:

■ Rack and sort boards *(page 70)* before you cut and install them. Choose the best-looking side to face up and return bad boards to the lumberyard.

■ Drill a pilot hole if driving a fastener less than 3 inches from the end of a board. Otherwise the board may split.

■ Keep in mind that when you do the chalk-line cut, your circular saw cannot reach all the way to the house. Cut the board or two that will be nearest the house before you install them *(page 71)*.

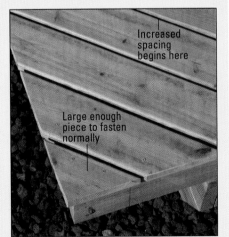

■ Once you're within 3 feet of a corner, measure to see how wide the last piece will be. If it looks like you'll end up with a tiny corner piece, try avoiding it by increasing the spacing between the last four or five boards.

WHAT IF...
You're stuck with a small piece?

If the last piece is large enough (as shown at left), install it as you did the other boards, by drilling pilot holes and driving fasteners down through the face of the board. If the piece is small, cut and attach it after making the chalk line cuts. Drill horizontal pilot holes and attach the piece with screws or nails driven into the adjoining deck board (above). There will be no space between these two boards.

SIMPLE STAIRS

For complete instructions on planning and building stairs, see *pages 73–79.* However, if the deck is less than 2 feet above grade and you need only a set of standard steps, you can simplify the process. A standard step has a rise (vertical distance) of 6 to 8 inches and a run (horizontal distance) of 10 to 12 inches.

You may choose to end the stairs with a landing, made of either concrete *(pages 76–77)* or patio pavers *(page 99).* Or you can suspend the steps (as shown here) above the ground until the landing is installed.

Home centers sell precut stringers. This is the simplest solution if you need only a few steps. These usually have 7-inch rises and 11-inch runs. Cut the top of a precut stringer to fit against the deck joist *(page 74).* You may need to cut the bottom so that the last step is shorter than the others.

The method shown on this page works if you have one or two steps. You can adapt the dimensions to suit your site. If possible, make all the steps (including the bottom step) the same height.

PRESTART CHECKLIST

☐ **TIME**
Once the landing is installed, a couple of hours to construct and attach a simple step or two.

☐ **TOOLS**
Tape measure, circular saw, drill, hammer, carpenter's level, layout square

☐ **SKILLS**
Figuring rise and run for a couple of steps, measuring and cutting boards, fastening with nails or screws

☐ **MATERIALS**
Lumber for framing and treads, hurricane ties, stake

1 Build a simple box frame for the step from 2×6 or 2×8 pressure-treated lumber. If the treads are ⁵⁄₄ decking, add a cross support every 16 inches; if they're 2×s, add a support every 24 inches. Attach the box to the outside joist with hurricane ties and add a stake to avoid wracking.

2 Cut the treads to length and fasten them in place using 2-inch fasteners for ⁵⁄₄-inch decking (shown above) or 3-inch fasteners for 2× treads.

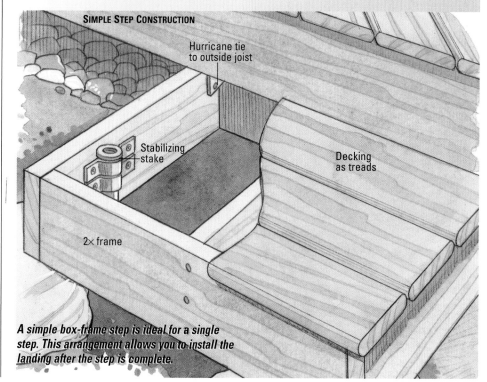

SIMPLE STEP CONSTRUCTION

Hurricane tie to outside joist

Stabilizing stake

Decking as treads

2× frame

A simple box-frame step is ideal for a single step. This arrangement allows you to install the landing after the step is complete.

BENCH WITH PLANTERS

Some deck planters are wood containers that actually hold soil. Others serve as decorative containers into which you can place potted plants. The type shown here combines the features of both: an attractive planter box that holds a large plastic tub with holes in the bottom for drainage.

Tubs are available at garden or home centers. Another option is to order a galvanized liner from a sheet-metal shop; the liner can be custom-made to fit any size planter.

Whichever type of planter you choose to make, be sure that water can drain freely out of the bottom and plan where that water will go. If drained water gets trapped in a cavity below the planter, it could cause decking to rot. Most decorative plants need less than 1 foot of soil depth. Rather than loading a tall planter with unnecessary soil, build a shelf inside.

A bench is even simpler than a planter. A platform that is 16 inches wide and 17 inches high will be comfortable for most people.

PRESTART CHECKLIST

☐ **TIME**
Several hours to build two planters and a bench

☐ **TOOLS**
Tape measure, level, drill, hammer, circular saw, layout square, framing square, squeeze or pipe clamps

☐ **SKILLS**
Measuring and cutting boards, fastening with nails or screws

☐ **PREP**
Purchase a liner and design a planter to fit around it

☐ **MATERIALS**
Lumber for the planter and the bench, screws or nails, L-shape strap ties with screws, 6-inch carriage bolts

Leave equal spaces of at least 1" on each side

1 Cut pieces of ⁵⁄₄ decking to serve as the vertical side pieces. To build each side, clamp the pieces side by side and attach a 2×6 brace, which also acts as a cleat to hold the bottom pieces (Step 2). Cut the brace 2 inches shorter than the width of the side and attach it with screws.

Cleat

Shelf for container

2 Hold three of the sides together with clamps and drive nails or screws to fasten them together. Attach the fourth side in the same way. Cut pieces of decking for the shelf. Check the structure for square, then attach the shelf pieces to the cleat. Add the top and bottom trim pieces.

PLANTER CONSTRUCTION

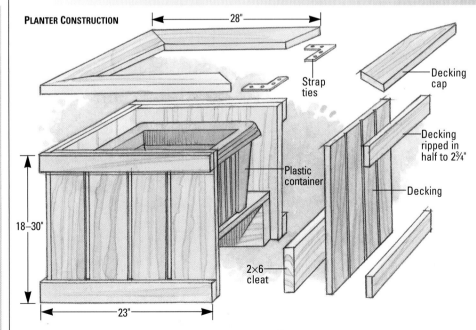

28"

Strap ties

Decking cap

Decking ripped in half to 2¾"

Plastic container

Decking

18–30"

2×6 cleat

23"

This simple planter is made primarily of pressure-treated ⁵⁄₄×6 decking. Vary height and width to suit your deck. The cleat can be set to suit the height of the plant container you'll use. Trim pieces can be butt jointed or mitered.

3 To make the cap, cut decking boards at 45-degree miters and assemble using L-shape strap ties. The frame should overhang the top trim pieces by 1½ inches on all sides. Set the liner in the box and then fasten the cap using 2-inch deck screws sunk into the top trim piece.

4 Toe-fasten the planters in position with 3-inch fasteners. For each bench, measure between two planters and construct a 2×4 frame with crosspieces every 2 feet or so. Set the finished frame between the planters and fasten it into the planters with four 3-inch fasteners.

5 If a seat is longer than 8 feet, add 4×4 supports every 6 feet or so. Cut seat pieces out of decking lumber and fasten them to the frame with screws or nails driven into the joists. Space the seat pieces as you would decking and allow them to overhang the frame by 1 or 2 inches.

BENCH CONSTRUCTION

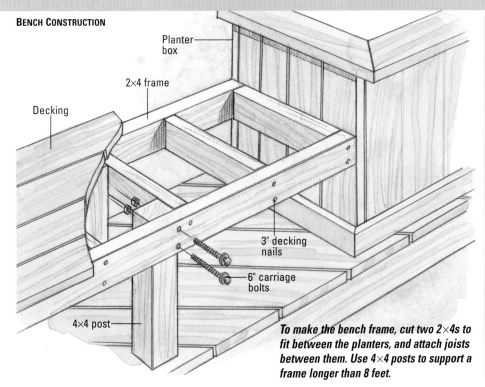

To make the bench frame, cut two 2×4s to fit between the planters, and attach joists between them. Use 4×4 posts to support a frame longer than 8 feet.

REFRESHER COURSE
Toe-fastening posts

To attach the posts and the planters to the deck, drive toenails or angled screws. Drill a pilot hole 2 inches above the deck at about a 60-degree angle. Install a 3-inch deck screw or 16d nail.

DECK ON A SLOPED SITE
STAIRS & RAILING

A rectangular deck attached to the house is quick to build and makes efficient use of materials. The angled corner adds an attractive, space-saving feature that requires only about half a day in extra labor.

Framing the deck
A ledger board provides an ideal starting place for framing a deck. Because the ledger is attached to the house, it's easy to make sure the framing is the correct height and length.

Once the ledger is set, reference down from it to the ground and lay out the post locations. Where the deck has an angled corner, two posts must be placed at a corresponding angle. Fortunately these two footings can be off by an inch or two without weakening the deck structure.

The beam in this design rests on top of the posts. You may prefer (or your building inspector may require) a sandwich-type beam; see *page 44*. This deck uses the simplest type of beam, made by fastening two 2×10s together.

Building stairs
If the deck is only 1 or 2 feet above fairly level ground, you can build simple stairs using precut stringers available at home centers. If the deck is higher or the ground slopes, careful planning is required to make sure that all the steps (including the bottom one) are the same height. This chapter presents complete instructions on how to build the stairs.

Working on a slope
A site that slopes away from the house presents challenges for a deck builder. Extra care must be taken to ensure that posts are plumb and the deck is level.

If a slope is severe, special measures may be needed to keep the footings from slowly sliding down the hill. In extreme circumstances, the footings may have to be connected to the house's foundation; hire a professional for this type of work.

For safety and convenience, work with at least one helper whenever possible.

Working from a ledger attached to the house, here's how to cope with a sloped site.

CHAPTER PREVIEW

Anchoring a ledger
page 58

Laying out on a sloped site
page 62

Framing
page 64

Laying decking
page 70

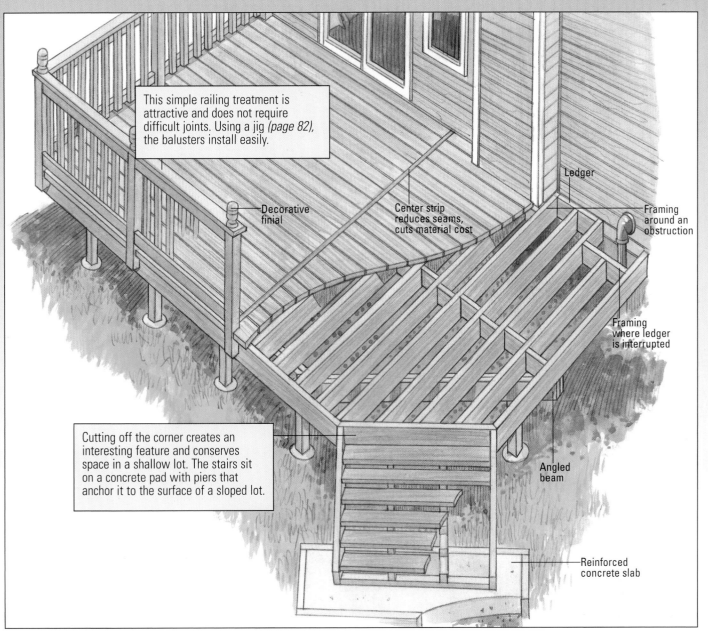

This simple railing treatment is attractive and does not require difficult joints. Using a jig *(page 82)*, the balusters install easily.

Decorative finial

Center strip reduces seams, cuts material cost

Ledger

Framing around an obstruction

Framing where ledger is interrupted

Angled beam

Cutting off the corner creates an interesting feature and conserves space in a shallow lot. The stairs sit on a concrete pad with piers that anchor it to the surface of a sloped lot.

Reinforced concrete slab

A deck installed on a sloped site calls for special layout techniques (pages 62–63) and often is more challenging to frame. A ledger provides a level starting point; its height and length are helpful reference points while you're laying out the posts, beams, and framing.

Laying out stairways
page 73

Forming a concrete pad
page 76

Building stairs
page 78

Adding a railing
page 80

ANCHORING A LEDGER

Most decks are attached to the house with a ledger because it easily adds strength to the structure. In some areas with unstable soil, however, a deck must be unattached to prevent damage to the house if it shifts (see *pages 34–49*).

Make it level and strong

The ledger will be the reference point for laying out the entire deck, so take time to position it precisely. If the siding or door is not level, you may be tempted to install the ledger out of level for appearance's sake. Resist the temptation: An angled ledger greatly complicates the rest of the construction process. A perfectly level ledger will ease the job of installing posts, beams, and joists.

Attach the ledger with large screws driven into framing members—not just into the house's sheathing. In most cases there will be an outside joist just below the door sill, which is where the ledger goes. Drill test holes to make sure the screws will have a hefty 2× board to grab.

PRESTART CHECKLIST

☐ **TIME**
Four to five hours to cut and install a 16-foot ledger board on a frame house; longer to attach to masonry

☐ **TOOLS**
Layout square, tape measure, level, circular saw, hammer, drill, socket wrench

☐ **SKILLS**
Measuring and cutting boards, testing for level, driving lag screws

☐ **PREP**
Draw the exact location of the ledger on the house

☐ **MATERIALS**
Ledger board(s), lag screws with washers, shims if necessary

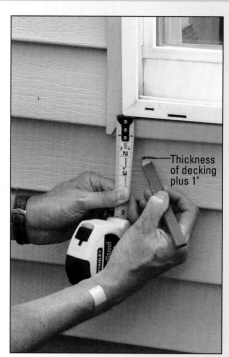

Level line

Thickness of decking plus 1"

1 To mark the top of the ledger, measure down from the bottom of the door sill the thickness of the decking plus 1 inch. This small step-down will keep most rain and melted snow from seeping through the threshold.

2 Using a carpenter's level or a water level and a straightedge *(page 30)*, carefully draw a level line on the house siding to indicate where the top of the ledger should be positioned.

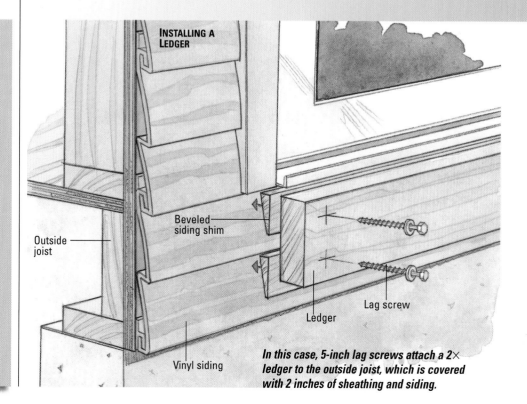

INSTALLING A LEDGER

Outside joist

Beveled siding shim

Lag screw

Ledger

Vinyl siding

In this case, 5-inch lag screws attach a 2×ledger to the outside joist, which is covered with 2 inches of sheathing and siding.

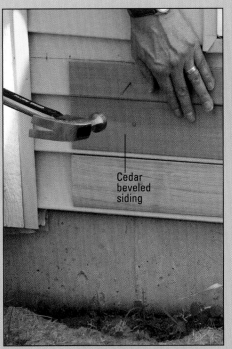

3 Mark for the outside edges of the ledger. On each side, the deck will extend past the ledger by 1½ inches (the thickness of the outside joist) plus the amount that the decking will overhang (in this case, another 1½ inches).

4 If you have beveled horizontal siding on your house, install pieces of cedar beveled siding to produce a flat surface for the ledger. You'll have to rip-cut the cedar *(page 29)* so its thickness matches the thickness of the house siding. Attach each piece with a nail every few feet.

5 If there is an existing concrete stairway, your inspector may want you to remove it. If you do not remove it, you'll need to cut the ledger to fit around it. Hold the ledger in place and mark for a cutout so that the ledger will rest on top of the concrete.

Setting a ledger into siding

In many areas it is common to cut and remove a section of siding and then set the ledger inside the cutout. The problem with this method is that it exposes the house's sheathing, which is not pressure-treated and is likely to rot if it gets wet. If your inspector requires this method, follow these steps:

■ Cut vinyl or wood siding using a circular saw with the blade set to cut just through the siding and no deeper. (For aluminum siding, turn the saw blade backward.)

■ Finish the cuts at the corners using a knife, a chisel, or tin snips.

■ Staple on a layer of tar paper to protect the sheathing.

■ Cut drip-cap metal flashing to fit and slide it up under the siding. The flashing must cover the top edge of the ledger.

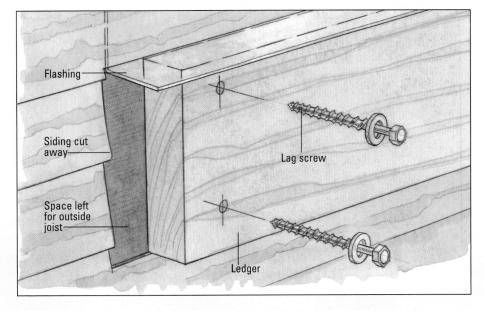

Anchoring a ledger (continued)

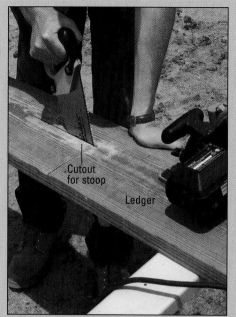

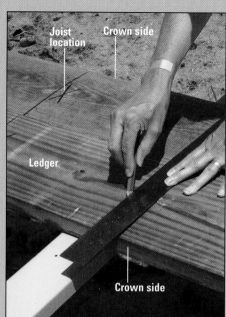

6 Cut the ledger board and the header joist to length. The header is usually 3 inches longer than the ledger. If you need to notch the ledger to go around an obstruction, first cut with a circular saw. Stop the cuts short of the corners to prevent overcutting. Finish the cuts with a handsaw.

7 Lay the ledger and header next to each other with their crowns *(page 17)* facing outward and the header overhanging the ledger by 1½ inches on each end. Mark both boards for joists, in this case every 16 inches. Mark a large X on the side of the line where the joist will go.

8 Have a helper or two hold the ledger in place while you drive 3-inch screws to hold it in place temporarily. Make sure the ledger has its crown side up. Test the ledger for level and adjust if necessary.

WHAT IF...
The ledger anchors to brick, block, or concrete?

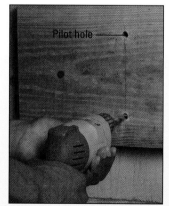

1 Drill the ledger for lag-screw pilot holes. Then use masonry screws or braces to hold it firmly in place while you drill locator holes with a small masonry bit.

2 Remove the ledger. Drill holes using a masonry bit that is the correct size for masonry anchors *(page 19)*. Drill at least ¼ inch deeper than the length of the anchors and blow out any dust.

3 Tap the masonry anchors into the holes until they are flush or slightly recessed.

4 Reposition the ledger and drive the lag screws into the anchors. Partially drive all the screws, then go back and tighten them all.

9 Check indoors to make sure lag screws will not hit any gas or water lines. Drill pilot holes for the lag screws. Place the holes where they will not get in the way of the joists. Drill a hole whose diameter is slightly less than the screw diameter through the ledger only.

10 Use a long bit to bore a smaller hole through the house framing. Slip a washer onto a lag screw and tap the screw partway into the hole. Tighten the screw with a socket wrench.

11 Every few feet along its length check the ledger's face to see that it is at least close to plumb. To make adjustments, try tightening one screw. If that doesn't work, loosen both screws, insert a shim at the bottom or top, and retighten.

Hold-off method

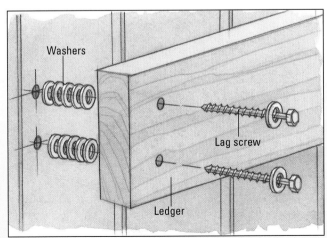

Some inspectors prefer that the ledger be held away from the siding with four or five washers so the ledger and siding can dry out quickly. Attach the ledger temporarily and drill all the pilot holes. Poke the screws through the ledger and slip on the washers. Insert the screw tips into the pilot holes and tighten the screws.

REFRESHER COURSE
Check the ledger for flatness

Once the ledger is installed, check to see whether it is straight or wavy along its length (page 88). If you cut all the joists the same length, any waves in the ledger will be duplicated in the header. If the ledger has no waves larger than ¼ or ½ inch, then build the outside frame and cut the joists to fit inside it, as shown on pages 62–69. If you have large waves, install the inside joists, cut them to length, and then install the header as shown on pages 91–92.

LAYING OUT ON A SLOPED SITE

To locate a deck's footings when the yard slopes away from the house, you must first measure out from the house along a level line, then down to the ground along a plumb line. This is difficult to do using standard string lines and batterboards. Instead, temporarily construct and support the deck's outside frame and then measure down for the footings.

This method may seem tedious, but actually it will not consume a lot of time. You must build the frame anyway, so you might as well do it now.

Though the supports are temporary, make them sturdy, because they need to hold the frame still while you work on it. You will reuse one of the supports later (Step 3, *page 68*). The 4×4s used as temporary supports can be used later as permanent posts for the deck.

PRESTART CHECKLIST

☐ **TIME**
Four or five hours to build a temporary frame, support it, and measure down to locate the footings

☐ **TOOLS**
Tape measure, framing square, mason's line, hammer, circular saw, drill, sledgehammer, plumb bob, post level, carpenter's level or water level

☐ **SKILLS**
Measuring and cutting boards, fastening with nails or screws, working on a slope

☐ **PREP**
Install the ledger; consult the framing plan to determine the exact dimensions for the outside joists and the header

☐ **MATERIALS**
Joist lumber, 16d galvanized nails or 3-inch deck screws, stakes, 4×4s for temporary supports, 1×4s for bracing

1 Cut the outside joists and the header to length. Lay the pieces on the ground and fasten the outside joists to the header with two or three screws or nails at each joint. Set the frame in position and check it for square, using both a framing square and the 3–4–5 method *(page 37)*. To keep the frame from going out of square, install a 1×4 brace at both corners and drive two screws into each joint. Use scraps of lumber to support the outside joists near the header, so they will be at the same height as the header.

PIER AND BEAM OVERVIEW

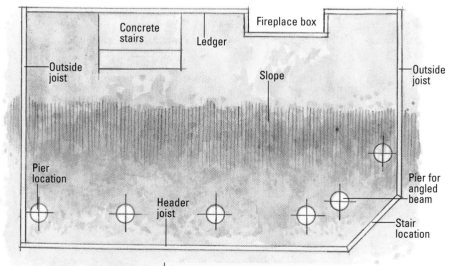

In this plan, four posts run in a row parallel to the house. At the angled corner, two posts are positioned at a 45-degree angle.

Piers for serious slopes
Codes require at least 7 horizontal feet of soil surrounding the bottom of the footing. If the ground past the footing is strongly inclined, an extra-deep hole may be needed.

2 To make a temporary support, place a piece of 1× lumber about 2 feet long on the sloped ground. Set a 4×4 post on top of the board, hold it plumb, and use a 2× scrap as a guide to mark its bottom for cutting, as shown. Cut the post and attach it to the board with screws.

3 Temporarily brace each support post with 1×4s and stakes. Raise the frame so it is level. Attach the outside joists to the ledger with one screw at each joint. Slide the temporary support up against the header

and anchor it with stakes as shown. Fasten the header to the support. Estimate the footing locations and install batterboards at both ends of the frame. Attach string lines to the batterboards.

STANLEY PRO TIP

Use a plumb bob

Use a plumb bob to position the string line so it runs through the middle of the footing locations. Measure along the string to find the locations of all the footings.

REFRESHER COURSE
Installing batterboards

Build batterboards. Make a batterboard out of 1×2 stakes and 1×4 or 1×3 crosspieces. Depending on the hardness of the soil and the slope, cut the stakes 16 to 36 inches long. Assemble the pieces with a single screw at each joint (see *page 34*).

Install batterboards and mason's line. Drive the stakes in until solid. Crosspieces should be at least 8 inches above ground. Locate batterboards at least 1 foot beyond the footing locations, so they won't get in the way when you dig the holes (see *page 35*).

FRAMING

Once you've laid out for the post holes, follow instructions on *pages 38–40* to dig and pour the footings. Footings should be at least 2 inches above grade at all points; on a sloped site, they'll stick up higher on the down side of the slope.

Keep things level, plumb, and straight
Take a little extra time to precisely align all the framing members. Double-check posts for plumb and adjust the braces if necessary. When using a mason's line to set a row of posts, keep the line about ⅛ inch away from the posts so the line stays straight. Framing members often get bumped during construction, so go back and check all the posts just before installing the beam, and check the beam just before installing the joists.

PRESTART CHECKLIST

☐ **TIME**
Two days with a helper to install posts, beams, and joists for a medium-size deck

☐ **TOOLS**
Tape measure, hammer, drill, circular saw, handsaw, layout square, chalk line, post level, carpenter's level, mason's line

☐ **SKILLS**
Measuring and cutting boards, checking for level and plumb, following a framing plan

☐ **PREP**
Install the footings with J-bolts and allow the concrete to set; draw layout lines on the ledger and the header

☐ **MATERIALS**
Lumber for posts, beams and joists, blocking, and braces; 16d galvanized nails or 3-inch deck screws, joist hangers, hurricane ties

A. Posts and beams

1 Install post anchors on the footings *(page 42)*. Estimate the height of the posts. Cut them about a foot longer than needed. Install and brace the outside posts so they are plumb in both directions. Run a mason's line to align the interior posts and adjust the bracing so the posts line up.

2 Hold a carpenter's level on top of a straight board. Set one end of the board on top of the ledger and hold the other against an outside post. Draw a mark on the post that is level with the top of the ledger.

FRAMING OVERVIEW

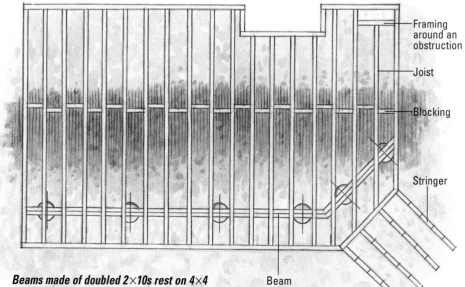

Beams made of doubled 2×10s rest on 4×4 posts and support 2×10 joists spaced 16 inches apart. The beam turns a 45-degree angle at the corner near the stairs.

3 To determine the height at which the post should be cut, measure down twice: Use a scrap piece of joist lumber to measure down the width of the joists and a scrap piece of beam lumber to measure down the width of the beam.

4 Measure down for the post height on the outside posts. Then snap a chalk line to mark the interior posts for cutting. For the posts that will support the angled beam, use a carpenter's level to mark for cutting.

5 To cut a post, mark all four sides with a layout square and cut with a circular saw. If the post is a 6×6, you'll need to finish the cut with a handsaw.

REFRESHER COURSE
Beam options

Beams for decks are usually made of 2× lumber, rather than a single piece of 4× lumber. (Thick lumber is more prone to cracks and warping than two or three 2×s fastened together.)

The simplest method of beam construction is shown on *page 66:* Just fasten two 2×s together. Drive two or three 10d nails or 2½-inch screws every 16 inches, unless your inspector specifies otherwise. The resulting beam is 3 inches thick, whereas the post bracket is 3½ inches thick. To make up the difference, add a small piece of ½-inch plywood (a shim) at the post *(page 66).*

Beam with spacers. Beams that will be set on posts should have pointed pressure-treated plywood spacers to increase rigidity and allow water and debris to fall through. Locate the spacers 12 to 18 inches apart. Some inspectors prefer a continuous strip of plywood the same width as the 2×s for added strength.

Two-part beam. A two-part beam is made by attaching 2×s to both sides of the posts, then cutting the posts. See *pages 89–90* for instructions. Because this method adds lateral stability to the deck, it is often used for second-story decks with long posts.

A. Posts and beams (continued)

6 Make the beams longer than they need to be (you'll trim them later). Lay one 2× on top of another with the crowns facing the same direction and the cupped sides *(page 16)* facing each other. To keep the top edges flush, you may need to use clamps. Drive two or three 10d nails or 2½-inch screws every 16 inches unless your building codes have specific fastening requirements.

7 One end of each beam is cut at a 45-degree angle. Cut only this end now; you'll cut the other end after the joists are installed and the frame is squared up. Set a circular saw blade at 45-degree angle (test it for accuracy on a scrap). Using a layout square as a guide, cut through one of the boards. Flip the beam over. Use a square to mark the other board with the same angle. Complete the cut.

WHAT IF...
The bracket is wider than the beam?

Because a beam of two 2×s is only 3 inches thick and the post bracket is 3½ inches wide, add a shim to make a secure join. Set the beams in place, and adjust them so they meet at the angle. At each post, shim out with a piece of ½-inch pressure-treated plywood about 4 inches by 6 inches.

STANLEY PRO TIP: **Brace the beam**

You'll prevent problems if you secure the beam as soon as you've plumbed and leveled it—otherwise it's easy to knock it out of position.

Temporarily brace the beam every 6 feet or so. To make a brace, drive a stake about 5 feet away from the beam on the up side of the slope. Anchor a 2×4 brace to the stake. Check the beam for plumb and drive a screw through the brace into the beam.

This is the best time to tighten the nuts that hold the post anchors to the concrete pier. Don't crank down too hard. You might need to refine your adjustments later.

B. Angled corner and joists

Equal distance in both directions

1 The joint where the two beams meet doesn't have to be tight, but the two beams must be on exactly the same level. Wedge shim above the post of one beam, if necessary. Drill pilot holes and drive screws or nails to fasten the beams to each other.

2 Assemble the outside frame as you did when you laid out the deck *(pages 62–63)*, set it on the beams, and attach the outside joists to the ledger. Check for square, then anchor the outside joists to the beam with screws. To mark for cutting the angle, measure out from the corner an equal distance in both directions. Align a straight board with both measurements and mark the header and the outside joist for 45-degree cuts. Transfer the marks to the faces of the boards.

WHAT IF…
Joists must be notched for steps?

Measure from the top of the ledge.

Mark for notching joist

2× support

1 If a set of concrete steps is in the way, notch the joists. Cut a joist to length and hold it in place. Level the joist. Steps often slope away from the house so there may be a gap under the joist. Mark where the joist meets the top of the ledger. Transfer that measurement to the joist where it crosses the edge of the step. Lay out your cut line between these two points.

2 Because the width of the joist has been reduced, it must be reinforced. Cut a scrap piece of 2× lumber to rest on a lower step and come up nearly to the top of the joist. Attach the support to the joist with several screws.

B. Angled corner and joists *(continued)*

3 Use one of the temporary supports that you made for marking the layout *(page 63)* to hold up the header; the outside joist rests on a beam. Set a circular saw to cut a 45-degree bevel and cut the header and the outside joist.

4 Measure between the corner cuts and cut an angled piece to fill the corner. Hold the angle-cut piece in place and drill pilot holes. Attach it with nails or screws.

STANLEY PRO TIP: **Trim beams when framing is complete**

1 Cut partway with a circular saw. Once the framing is complete and you've rechecked it for square, mark the beams for cutting off both ends. Remove the outside joist so you can make a clean cut. Cut with a circular saw to cut as deep as possible (here, at a 45-degree angle).

2 Complete the cut with a handsaw. Because a standard circular saw blade will probably not reach through both boards, finish the cut with a handsaw. If the resulting edge is ragged and unattractive, use a file or belt sander to smooth it out.

Measure for 16" center

Mark for angled cut

Hold end firmly against ledger

Skewed joist hanger

5 Cut and install the joists (see *pages 48–49*) with the crown up. Attach joist hangers at the ledger. At the other end use joist hangers, or screws or nails through the header into the joists. To measure for cutting a joist at the angled section, hold it in place and mark: Have a helper hold one end up against the ledger so that its bottom edge is close to the top of the ledger. While another helper measures to see that the joist is parallel with the next joist, mark the bottom of the joist. Transfer the mark to the face of the joist using a layout square and cut at a 45-degree angle.

6 Even if you have fastened all the other joists to the header by back-screwing or back-nailing, use a special "skewed" joist hanger to attach a joist at an angle.

WHAT IF...
You have to frame around an obstruction?

It's common for pipes, vent caps, and other obstructions to stick out of the house at about the same height as the ledger. If a vent falls right in the middle of the ledger, remove the vent cap and adapt the duct work to extend it out another 1½ inches. Use a hole saw to make a clean circular cut in the ledger, fit the duct through the ledger, and reinstall the vent cap *(page 87)*.

If a small pipe falls near the top or bottom of the ledger, simply cut a notch in the ledger and strengthen the ledger with extra fasteners on either side of the pipe.

If the obstacle is in the path of a joist, you'll have to frame around it, as shown at right. Install ledger pieces on either side, taking care that the pieces are at exactly the same height. Install joists on either side of the obstacle, then cut and install a piece of blocking between the joists. Cut a joist to run from the header to the blocking piece.

Sump pump outlet

Ledger

Joist

LAYING DECKING

If possible, buy decking boards long enough to span the entire deck so you won't need to make butt joints. If that is not possible, plan the location of the joints. Either place them in an alternating pattern or aim for randomness to hide them. Never place joints side by side. Wherever there will be a butt joint, double the nailing surface by fastening a 2×4 cleat alongside the joist *(page 24)*. To avoid joints, consider using a divider strip (below right).

Cut the decking to overhang the framing by 1½ inches. If you plan to attach lattice skirting framed by 1× (see *pages 104–105*), overhang the decking by 2½ inches.

These pages show installation of fairly dry cedar decking boards, using nails as spacers. Pressure-treated decking that is wet (see *page 17*) will shrink in width, so you may want to install the pieces tightly against each other. An experienced lumber retailer will tell you how wet the decking is.

To install decking at an angle, see *pages 50–52;* for a pattern that uses a center strip, see *pages 94–97*.

Crown faces house.

Good side up

1 Rack and sort seven or eight decking boards. Place them good-side-up on the framing. Orient each board with its crown facing the house. Choose an especially straight board for the first one, which goes up against the house.

2 Snap a chalk line that is the width of a decking board plus ½ inch away from the house. The siding may be a little wavy, so check that the line is at no point closer to the house than the width of a decking board.

PRESTART CHECKLIST

☐ **TIME**
A day to install decking for a 300- to 400-square-foot deck

☐ **TOOLS**
Tape measure, circular saw, chalk line, hammer, nail set, drill, chisel, flat pry bar

☐ **SKILLS**
Cutting with a circular saw, fastening with screws or nails, straightening boards

☐ **PREP**
Check that the framing is completely fastened and that there will be a nailing surface for all decking boards

☐ **MATERIALS**
Decking boards, screws or nails

Driving nails

Many people like the appearance of a nailhead better than a screw head. However, when driving nails, one wrong swing will make a permanent dent in the decking. Practice on scrap pieces until you get the knack. Aim for a free, easy swing with a fairly loose wrist. Use a hammer with a face that is smooth, not serrated. Finish driving nails with a nail set.

Avoid unsightly joints with a divider strip

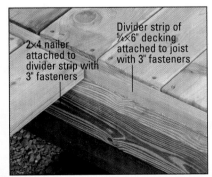

2×4 nailer attached to divider strip with 3" fasteners

Divider strip of ⁵⁄₄×6" decking attached to joist with 3" fasteners

If your deck is longer than 16 feet and you want to avoid unsightly joints, here's a nifty solution: In the center of the deck, attach a piece of decking to the joist using 3-inch fasteners. Attach a 2×4 cleat to the piece of decking. Butt the decking boards up against the divider strip on either side, leaving a ⅛-inch gap for expansion.

3 Cut the first decking board to length now, because you cannot cut it when you make the chalk-line cut (see Step 8). Align the board with the chalk-line marks and attach it with as many fasteners as it takes to keep the board straight. Drive the fasteners into the centers of the joists.

4 Allow succeeding boards to "run wild"— install them longer than they need to be so you can cut them off later. Use nails as spacers between the boards. Install as many fasteners as it takes to keep the boards straight. Drive the fasteners into the centers of joists.

5 To bend a warped board, drive a fastener partway into the decking (but not into the joist). Have a helper push it into position and finish driving the fastener. Every seven boards or so, sight along a board or use a string line to check that the decking is straight. Make adjustments if necessary.

STANLEY PRO TIP

Pilot holes near a board end

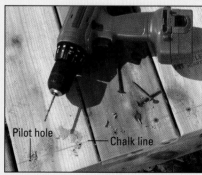

Wherever a fastener will be less than 3 inches from the end of a board, take a few seconds to drill a pilot hole before driving the fastener. If you fail to do this, chances are good that the board will split—a condition that cannot be repaired.

INVISIBLE DECK FASTENERS

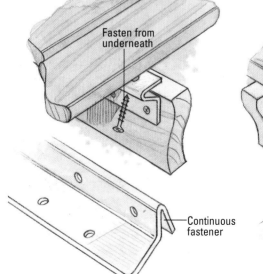

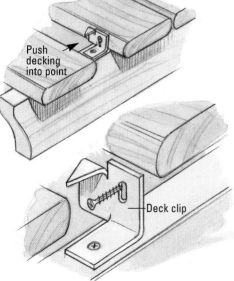

Avoid the appearance of nail or screw heads by installing a continuous fastener or deck clips. Though these methods are more expensive and take longer to install than nails or screws, many people consider them worth the trouble. Deck clips can be installed while you're working on top of the deck; continuous fasteners require driving screws from underneath.

Laying decking (continued)

Header

Install fasteners along chalk line.

Chalk line

6 When you are within five or six boards of the edge, measure to see whether the last piece will overhang the header an acceptable amount—¾ inch to 2½ inches. If not, you may need to rip-cut the last piece. Or increase or decrease the spacing to make up the difference *(page 52)*.

7 Once all the boards are installed, using as few fasteners as possible, snap chalk lines over the centers of joists and drive fasteners along the lines. This will produce lines of fastener heads that are straight, with only a few exceptions—a crisp finishing touch.

8 Snap chalk lines 1½ inches outside the framing. Cut the lines with a circular saw. If any waste piece is longer than 16 inches, have a helper support it as you cut. Otherwise it could crack near the end of the cut. Cut freehand (as shown) or use a guide (see *page 52*).

Striking a chalk line

To measure 1½ inches away from the framing, hold a piece of 2× lumber under the decking and mark the decking at both ends of the cut. Have a helper hold the chalk line at one mark while you pull it taut over the other. Lift straight up on the line and let go to create a straight line. If the line is incomplete, repeat the process.

WHAT IF...
Decking must be notched?

If you have to cut decking to go around a long outcropping such as a threshold, a step, or the second level of a deck, you may have to cut a long notch.

Begin by holding the board against the outcropping. Mark both sides for the width of the cut. Measure how far the board must travel toward the outcropping (include the spacing between boards). This is the depth of the notch.

To cut the width, make a plunge cut. Set the blade deep enough to cut the board, plus ¼ inch. Retract the blade guard, start the motor, and lower the blade onto the cut line. Cut the face of the board first, just up to the cut lines. Then cut the bottom side, going a little past the cut lines. Finish with a handsaw.

LAYING OUT STAIRWAYS

Designing a stairway can be complicated and confusing. The trickiest part is making sure that all the steps—including the bottom and top steps—are the same height. A professional carpenter might consider the methods shown on the following pages to be slow, but they provide a nearly fail-safe approach for a do-it-yourselfer.

Stair options

The illustration at right shows the components of most deck stairways. A standard set of stairs has rises of about 7 inches and runs of 11 inches, but you may want deeper stairs (see *page 74* for options). If the treads will be 2×s, stringers can be spaced as much as 28 inches apart; if you will use decking boards, space stringers 18 inches apart or closer. Interior stringers must be notched; outside stringers may be notched or closed. For each tread, use a single 2×12 or 2×10, or use two or more boards spaced as you would decking boards. Risers (see *page 99)* are not necessary, but they do hide the underside of the deck and offer a more finished look.

PRESTART CHECKLIST

☐ **TIME**
A couple of hours to partially cut a stringer, calculate rise and run, and design a stairway

☐ **TOOLS**
Level, circular saw, tape measure, calculator, framing square with set stops, carpenter's pencil

☐ **SKILLS**
Basic mathematics, measuring and cutting, checking for level

☐ **PREP**
Finish the decking, and decide on the type of landing (if any)

☐ **MATERIALS**
Straight board, 2×12 for the first stringer

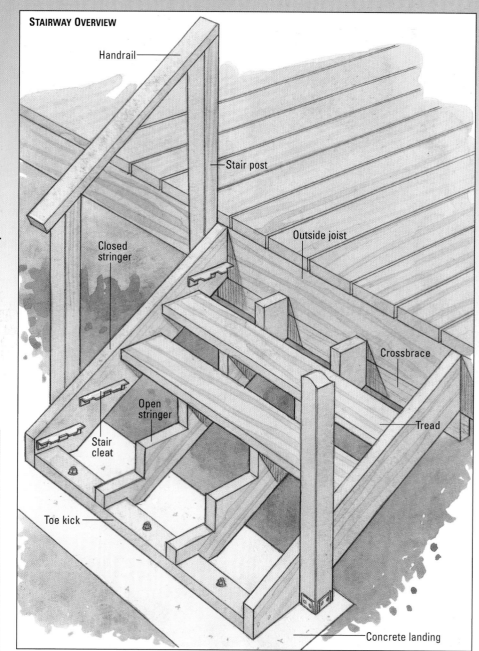

STAIRWAY OVERVIEW

Handrail

Stair post

Closed stringer

Outside joist

Crossbrace

Open stringer

Tread

Stair cleat

Toe kick

Concrete landing

The vertical distance that a stairway travels from the landing pad to the top of the deck is the **total rise.** The horizontal distance it travels is the **total run.** The vertical and horizontal distances traveled by each step are the **unit rise** and **unit run.**

A landing must be level (even if the yard is not) and may be made of concrete, pavers, or crushed stone. Stringers are the stair's joists, and these may be either notched or closed, with brackets. Stringers must be firmly attached to the deck; an extra brace (page 98) may be needed. A toe kick anchors the stringers to the landing pad. Treads—which may be composed of a single board or several pieces—are the part that you walk on. Optional risers (page 99) cover the vertical spaces between treads.

Laying out stairways *(continued)*

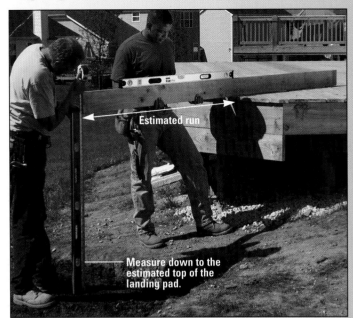

1 If the yard is level, find the total rise simply by measuring down from the deck to the ground. If the yard slopes, use a level and a long board to extend the deck level out to a point where you estimate that the stairway will end and measure down from there. Calculate rise and run. You may decide that you need to move the landing pad closer to or farther from the deck. If so, repeat this step and recalculate.

2 Once you've determined the unit rise and run as well as the number of rises, draw a stringer on a 2×12. A framing square equipped with stair gauges (also called set stops) makes this easy. For the top and bottom of the stringer, remember to take into account the thickness of the treads.

Figuring rise and run

For ease of stepping, the deeper a stair's tread, the shorter its rise should be. The standard formula is: Twice the riser height plus the run should equal between 24 and 27 inches. (For example, if rises are 7 inches and runs are 11 inches, 2 times 7 equals 14, plus 11 equals 25.)

To calculate rise and run, measure the total rise (Step 1, above) and divide by the unit rise that you desire. Round off to the nearest whole number; this is the number of rises. Then divide the total rise by the number of rises to find the exact rise for each step. For example, you want unit rises of about 7 inches and runs of 11 inches. If, as shown here, the total rise is 58 inches, divide 58 by 7 to get 8.28. Round that down to 8 rises.

Divide 8 rises into 58, to find the precise unit rise, 7.25 (7¼) inches. Multiply the desired unit run by the number of rises, minus one (remember, the last rise is up to the deck surface), in this case 7×11 = 77. So the stairway will end 77 inches away from the deck.

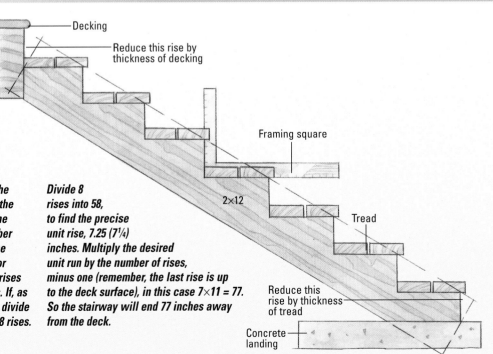

Top cut

Do not cut treads yet.

Bottom cut line

Check tread mark for level.

Stake marks stringer location.

3 Double-check the stringer layout, thinking through how it will go together. The bottom rise should be 1½ inches shorter than the other rises if you are using 2× treads, and 1 inch shorter if you are using ⁵⁄₄ decking for treads. Visualize how the stringer will attach to the deck (see *page 79*). Cut the stringer at both ends only.

4 Hold the partially cut stringer against the deck in the position where it will be attached. Check that the treads will be level. Mark the ground for the location and height of the landing pad. The landing pad should support the stringers fully and should extend outward a comfortable distance for walking.

WHAT IF...
You want to install the pad later?

If a stairway will not be heavily used, it can end at the yard with no landing pad. Or you can build the stairway first and add a pad under the stringers later. Calculate rise and run as you normally would and cut the stringers *(page 78),* keeping them 1 or 2 inches above grade at their bottoms. Temporarily support the stringers at their bottoms, attach them to the deck, and check that they are square to the deck and that their treads are level.

STRINGERS WITHOUT A PAD

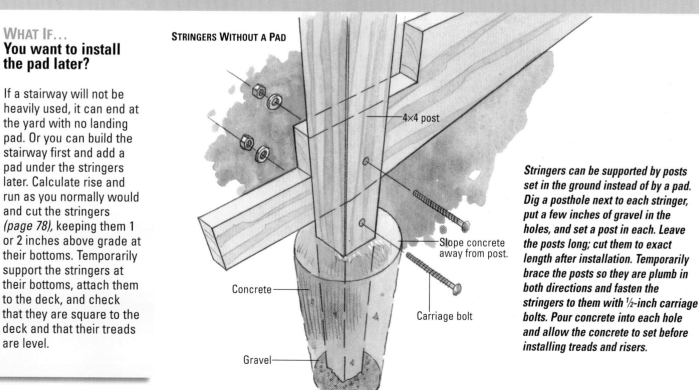

4×4 post

Slope concrete away from post.

Concrete

Carriage bolt

Gravel

Stringers can be supported by posts set in the ground instead of by a pad. Dig a posthole next to each stringer, put a few inches of gravel in the holes, and set a post in each. Leave the posts long; cut them to exact length after installation. Temporarily brace the posts so they are plumb in both directions and fasten the stringers to them with ½-inch carriage bolts. Pour concrete into each hole and allow the concrete to set before installing treads and risers.

FORMING A CONCRETE PAD

Many concrete patios and sidewalks are less than 2 inches thick and lack metal reinforcing. In areas with freezing winters, they will almost certainly develop cracks. These pages show how to build a long-lasting pad.

A concrete slab may be raised one step's height above the yard or the adjacent patio surface, or it can be set just above ground level. Unless the pad is larger than 75 square feet, there is no need to worry about drainage. *Pages 74–75* show how to figure the location and height of a landing for steps. The pad shown here includes two piers to "key" into its sloped site. Omit the piers if you have a level site.

Though it may feel solid a few hours after pouring, concrete takes a week or two to achieve full strength. Wait at least three days before exerting heaving pressure on the pad.

PRESTART CHECKLIST

☐ **TIME**
  About a day to excavate, build forms, mix concrete, pour, and finish the surface

☐ **TOOLS**
  Level, tape measure, circular saw, sledgehammer, drill, hammer, wire cutters, concrete, wheelbarrow, hoe, concrete finishing tools *(page 77)*

☐ **SKILLS**
  Measuring and cutting, checking for level and square, mixing in a wheelbarrow, smoothing a concrete surface

☐ **PREP**
  Determine the location for the pad and remove any sod

☐ **MATERIALS**
  Lumber for forms and stakes, gravel, bags of dry-mix concrete, reinforcing wire mesh

Drive stakes below the top of the form boards.

1 Excavate topsoil and tamp down about 2 inches of gravel. Cut 2× boards to use as forms for the pad. Fasten them together in a rectangle. Use a framing square to check the corners for square. Fasten the boards to stakes driven into the ground and check for level and square.

Reinforcing mesh

2 Backfill with soil behind the form boards so wet concrete can't ooze out from the bottom. Cut wire reinforcing mesh to fit and lay it on top of stones so that it will be near the center of the pad's thickness when you pour the concrete.

FORMING AND POURING A CONCRETE PAD

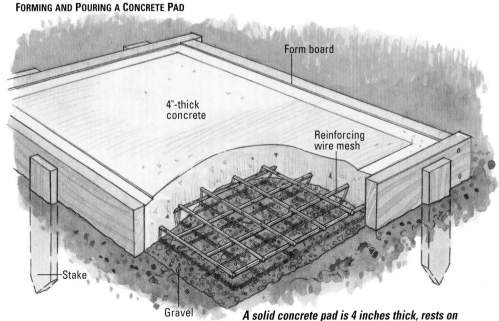

Form board

4"-thick concrete

Reinforcing wire mesh

Stake

Gravel

A solid concrete pad is 4 inches thick, rests on a bed of well-tamped gravel, and is reinforced with special reinforcing wire mesh.

Screed board

3 Mix the concrete in a wheelbarrow *(page 39)* and pour it into the forms. Using a board long enough to reach from form to form, screed the surface: Drag the board, using a side-to-side motion as you move it across the length of the pad. Repeat until the surface is fairly level and has no low spots.

4 Using a wooden, steel, or magnesium float (shown below), smooth out the entire area. With the float held nearly flat, lightly scrape across the pad in long, sweeping arcs. As you work, water will rise to the top. Keep smoothing as long as the surface is wet. Once it has started to dry, lightly drag a broom across it to create a nonslip surface.

Concrete finishing tools

Magnesium float

Mason's trowel

Edger

These three tools are all you need to finish a small concrete pad. A magnesium float is easier to use than a steel or wooden float and is more than adequate for smoothing the concrete before giving it a broom finish (see Step 4 above).

5 Slip the point of a mason's trowel between the form and the concrete and slice all around the pad to a depth of 1 to 2 inches.

Edger

6 Run an edger around the perimeter to round off the corners. This will prevent chipping. Press lightly and repeat until the corners are smooth. Once the concrete has set for 1 day, pry away the forms.

BUILDING STAIRS

Once you've determined the rise and run *(pages 73–75)* and have installed a landing *(pages 76–77)*, you're ready to build the stairs.

Stairs have to withstand plenty of use, so choose lumber that is straight and free of knots and other defects. Pay extra for "select" or "No. 1" lumber. Some lumber sources sell 2×12s specifically approved for use as treads or stringers.

If you accidentally break off a stringer's "tooth," don't be alarmed. Drill pilot holes, apply exterior grade polyurethane glue, and drive screws or nails to reattach it.

The full width of the stringers must be firmly attached to the deck framing. Usually the outside or header joist is not deep enough, so you need to install a 2×6 or 2×8 brace directly below. This may require some improvising. Build out from the beam or from the posts so that the brace is as strong as the joist above it (see *pages 98*).

PRESTART CHECKLIST

☐ **TIME**
Once the landing is finished and the layout calculated, 4 to 5 hours to cut and install stringers, a toe kick, treads, risers, and rail posts for an 8-step stairway

☐ **TOOLS**
Tape measure, level, hammer, drill, circular saw, handsaw, framing square, layout square

☐ **SKILLS**
Cutting 2× lumber at angles, fastening with nails or screws

☐ **PREP**
Complete the crossbrace, lay out and cut either end of a stringer, and install the landing

☐ **MATERIALS**
2×12 for stringers, 2× lumber or decking for treads, 2×4 toe kick, 4×4 posts, post anchors, angle brackets, screws or nails, masonry screws

1 Test the partially cut stringer *(page 75)* to make sure it fits between the deck and the landing with the tread lines level. With a circular saw, cut each line. Don't cut farther than the intersection of the tread and riser lines.

2 Finish the cuts with a handsaw or a saber saw. Take care not to bump the resulting teeth of the stringer. Use the first stringer as a template for cutting the others.

Notching the inside stringer

The bottom of an inside stringer rests partly on the slab and partly on the 2×4 toe kick *(page 73)*. Use a circular saw and handsaw to cut a notch 1½ inches high and 3½ inches deep.

WHAT IF…
A cleated stringer is used?

To make a closed stringer, make only one cut at the bottom and one at the top. Draw lines indicating both the bottom and top of the treads. Drill pilot holes and attach the tread cleats with 1¼-inch lag screws.

3 Attach a crossbrace directly below the outside or header joist and anchor the stringers to the brace. The tops of the notched stringers (and the metal cleats on closed stringers) must line up so a tread can rest across all of them. Use a framing square to check that the stringers are square to the deck and anchor them to the deck with angle brackets.

4 Slip a 2×4 toe kick under the inside stringers and against the insides of the outside stringers. Drill holes through the toe kick; then drill holes into the landing using a masonry bit. Set bolts and anchors or drive masonry screws to fasten the toe kick to the landing. Drill angled pilot holes and drive screws or nails to attach the stringers to the toe kick.

5 Attach a post anchor to the concrete positioned so the post can attach to the full width of the stringer. (Use the epoxy and threaded rod method shown on *page 42.*) Fasten the post to the anchor with screws. Plumb the post and drill a hole for a carriage bolt that will run through the post and stringer. Be sure the carriage bolt will not interfere with the tread or tread hardware. Tap the bolt through and fasten it with a washer and nut.

6 If the outside stringers are notched, cut the treads so they overhang 1½ inches on each side. If you are using closed stringers, cut treads to fit between them. Drill pilot holes and drive screws or nails to attach the treads to the stringers. Use three fasteners per joint for a 2×12 or 2×10 tread, two fasteners for narrower boards.

ADDING A RAILING

A railing is one of the most visible parts of a deck, so choose lumber that is free of any cracks and splinters. After the railing is installed, smooth all the corners with a hand sander.

Assembling the parts

Draw your design and double-check that you have the correct sizes and measurements. Balusters are as long as the height of the railing, minus the gap at the bottom (about 2 to 3 inches) and the thickness of the rail cap. Posts are as long as the height of the railing, plus the width of the joist and the thickness of the decking, minus the thickness of the rail cap.

Check codes for the following specs:
- The minimum height of the railing.
- How far apart the balusters can be.
- How the posts attach to the framing.
- The maximum space between the bottom of the balusters and the deck.

It may be possible to buy precut balusters and posts that fit your design requirements.

PRESTART CHECKLIST

☐ **TIME**
Working with a helper, about a day to build a railing for a medium-size deck

☐ **TOOLS**
Tape measure, hammer, drill, circular saw, power miter saw, saber saw, clamp, post level, ratchet and socket

☐ **SKILLS**
Accurate measuring and cutting, fastening with nails and screws

☐ **PREP**
Finish the framing and the decking

☐ **MATERIALS**
4×4s for posts, 2×4s for bottom and top rails, 2×2s for balusters, decking or 2×6s for rail cap, screws or nails, carriage bolts with washers and nuts, lag screws

A. Installing the post

1" from post side

1 Posts are as long as the height of the railing, plus the width of the joist and the thickness of the decking, minus the thickness of the rail cap. Set up a jig that allows you to cut all the posts to the correct length. A 22½-degree angle cut on the bottom end adds a decorative touch.

Jig for length of post

2 Mark for two holes in the posts that are each 1 inch from the side of the post and 1½ inches from the top or bottom of the joist. Drill holes that are the same diameter as the carriage bolts you will use (Step 4). Stagger the holes as shown above to avoid splitting along the grain lines.

RAILING OVERVIEW

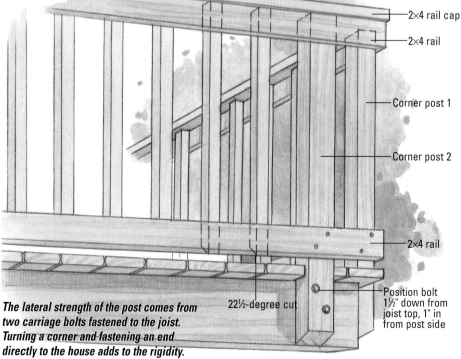

2×4 rail cap

2×4 rail

Corner post 1

Corner post 2

2×4 rail

22½-degree cut

Position bolt 1½" down from joist top, 1" in from post side

The lateral strength of the post comes from two carriage bolts fastened to the joist. Turning a corner and fastening an end directly to the house adds to the rigidity.

3 For each post, cut a notch in the decking so the post can fit tightly against the joist. Use a professional-quality saber saw for this—it's difficult to cut straight with a cheap model. Cut the notches with ⅛ inch of play to allow for expansion and so you won't have to force the post in.

4 Clamp the post so it is plumb in both directions. Drill into the existing holes and through the joist. Tap carriage bolts all the way through. Under the deck, slip on a washer and tighten a nut for each bolt.

5 Where the railing meets the house, use 5-inch lag screws and washers to firmly fasten a 2×4. This is stronger than a 4×4 post attached to the deck.

WHAT IF...
You want notched posts?

Notched posts take time and experience to cut but make a pleasing finishing touch for a deck railing. They draw the baluster up closer to the deck edge and make a slightly firmer joint than surface-mounted posts.

Mark the posts for a notch that is 1½ inches deep and as long as the depth of the joist—about 7½ inches for a 2×8 joist, about 9½ inches for a 2×10. (Use a joist scrap to be exact.) Add the thickness of the decking and mark for the crosscut.

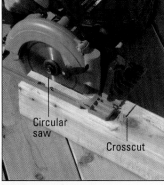

Cut the notch.
Make a crosscut where the notch ends. With the saw set to maximum depth, cut the long lines on each side without cutting beyond the crosscut. (For a corner post, set the blade to a depth of 1½ inches and make two long cuts.)

Chisel away the excess.
Use a hammer and chisel to crack out the waste—it will neatly pop out as one piece. Then chisel away the remnant where the saw blade could not reach.

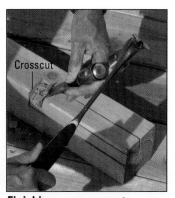

Finishing a corner post.
Make the long cuts and a shallow crosscut. Chisel toward the cross cut and split out the waste. Chisel down along the crosscut and along the long cuts to remove the remnant of wood remaining.

B. Installing the deck railing

1 Measure and cut pieces for the bottom rail. At an outside corner, hold two pieces in place and mark for a cut. If you have good carpentry skills, you could miter this corner. However, miter joints tend to come apart in time. A simple butt joint is safer.

2 Measure and mark the proper space between the bottom rail and the deck (check local building codes). Position the bottom rail; drive two nails or screws into each post. Install the top rails, top edges flush with the post tops. Drive two 3-inch fasteners where rails join at the corner.

3 Make a simple jig that supports the end of the baluster and stops it at the correct length. Test the jig to make sure your measurements are correct and then gang-cut the balusters as needed.

Adding the stair railing

1 For the top stair rail, hold a 2×4 against the top and bottom posts, parallel with the stairway. At the top, mark the rail for an angled cut. Still holding the stair rail in position, mark the lower rail post (Step 2) for an angle cut.

2 Use a layout square and T-bevel to mark lines around the rail post. Set a circular saw blade to a depth about ¼ inch more than the thickness of the post and cut both angled lines. Have a helper hold the post, gently lifting upward as the cut is finished.

3 Cut the bottoms of the stairway balusters at 22½ degrees—just like the deck balusters. Then hold a baluster plumb against the angled railing and mark the top angle. Gang cut the balusters and fasten them in place using a scrap 2×4 spacer.

2×2 bumper for height

Jig sets on top rail

2×4 for spacer

Crosspiece for plumb

Baluster

4 Use a jig like this to space and plumb balusters and position them at the right height. Every fifth baluster, check for plumb. Make incremental adjustments in the next few balusters as needed. Attach with one 3-inch screw or nail driven into the top and bottom rails.

2½" deck screw

Post

5 Install the rail cap so it overhangs the top rail and post by equal amounts on each side of the posts. Drive two 2½-inch fasteners into each post and one every 2 feet or so into the top rail.

6 At a corner make a precise miter joint where two pieces of cap rail meet. First, on one of the boards, cut the mitered end only, let the other end run wild. Check the fit of the miter. If the fit is good, cut the other end of the cap rail. Drill pilot holes and drive screws to draw the joint tight.

2" deck screw

4 Where the stairway rail cap meets the deck rail cap, hold a board in position and mark it alongside the post for a bevel cut. Adjust the angle on a circular saw and experiment on scraps until it is right. Attach the cap rail with 2½-inch screws.

WHAT IF...
Finials will be added?

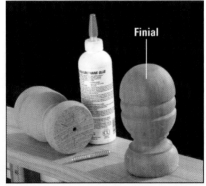

Finial

Typically, finials are placed above each post. Once the cap rail is in place, bore a hole ⅛-inch narrower than the double-threaded screw that comes with the finial. With pliers, twist the screw into the predrilled hole in the finial. Apply exterior-grade polyurethane glue to the bottom of finial and twist it into the cap rail.

STANLEY PRO TIP

Secret to a tight miter

Corners are seldom perfectly square; that's why even a well-executed miter joint will gap. To close the gap, clamp or tack the mitered cap rail in place. Then cut through the miter as shown. Push the pieces together and fasten for a perfect miter joint.

Two-Level Deluxe Deck

Wide Stairs & Pergola

This deck has attractive features that are easy to build. The decking of the upper level has an eye-catching chevron pattern. The stairway is extra wide—ideal for party seating. At one end of the deck, a pergola (an overhead trellis) is combined with a lattice screen to provide privacy.

Framing

While this deck's basic structure is similar to the others in this book, one difference is the beam: It is made of two 2×s bolted to both sides of the posts. This type of beam is generally easier to build than the beams shown in the other two decks, which rest on top of the posts.

Decking, stairs, and railing

A single strip of decking runs parallel to the house in the center of the upper level area. The other decking boards run at 45-degree angles and butt against the center strip. This method calls for extra framing—two rows of blocking—but once the center strip is installed, it's fairly easy to lay the rest of the decking.

Wide and deep stairs require more stringers and tread pieces, but the construction techniques are similar to those used in the basic stairs shown on Deck 2. The attractive paver landing is actually easier to build than pouring a plain concrete slab.

Each railing post is made of four pieces of 2× and 1× lumber. This is more complicated than installing simple 4×4s but requires only basic carpentry skills. The result is a decorative post that is less likely to crack than a solid 4×4. Once the posts are set, the balustrade sections can be built on the deck and then attached between the posts. Again, a little extra effort yields an upgraded look.

Pergola and trellis

A pergola made of several layers of beams, rafters, and top pieces is easy to build as long as you follow the step-by-step instructions. Trellis material comes in easy-to-cut 4×8 sheets and can be fastened in less than an hour.

Extra features often require no special skills and only a little extra time to build.

Chapter Preview

Laying out
page 86

Installing the beams
page 88

Installing joists
page 91

Decking with a center strip
page 94

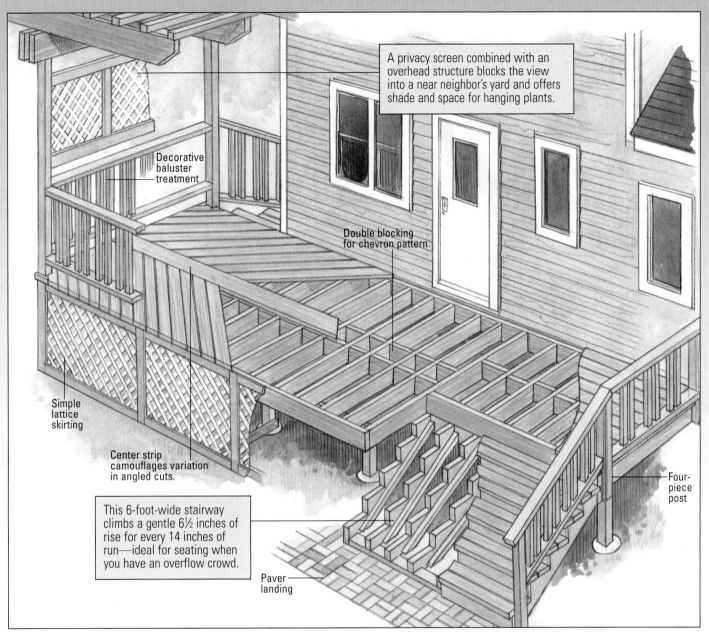

A privacy screen combined with an overhead structure blocks the view into a near neighbor's yard and offers shade and space for hanging plants.

Decorative baluster treatment

Double blocking for chevron pattern

Simple lattice skirting

Center strip camouflages variation in angled cuts.

This 6-foot-wide stairway climbs a gentle 6½ inches of rise for every 14 inches of run—ideal for seating when you have an overflow crowd.

Paver landing

Four-piece post

This is the most complicated deck in the book, packed with attractive features such as the extra-wide stairway, chevron-patterned decking, privacy screen with an overhead structure, and decorative skirting. Building these features requires only basic skills and a modest amount of additional time.

Building deep and wide stairs
page 98

Adding an upgraded railing
page 100

Building a pergola
page 102

Adding skirting
page 104

LAYING OUT

Aconcrete slab runs alongside this house—a fairly common situation. In some cases, it's feasible to lay joists directly on top of a slab. However, a slab is probably no more than 4 inches thick, so it cannot support posts.

The first step is to install one ledger for each level. (See *pages 58–61* for complete instructions.) The ledger should be positioned 1 inch plus the thickness of the decking below the bottom of the door sill. If the house has horizontal beveled siding, shim out with long pieces of cedar siding so that the ledgers will be vertically plumb *(page 59)*.

The footings and posts for the upper level of this deck are set in the ground beyond the slab; see *pages 34–37* for how to lay out the site with batterboards. The photos at right show laying out for the lower-level post, which will be set on piers that go through the slab.

PRESTART CHECKLIST

☐ **TIME**
Once the ledger is installed, several hours to build batterboards, run string lines and check them for square, and mark the slab for the footing locations

☐ **TOOLS**
Tape measure, hammer, sledgehammer, carpenter's level, drill, chalk line, mason's line, a jackhammer if a concrete patio is in the way

☐ **SKILLS**
Building batterboards, measuring, checking lines for square

☐ **PREP**
Install the ledger boards

☐ **MATERIALS**
1×2 and 1×4 for batterboards, a straight board, deck screws

Plumb down from this point

Shim extends 1½" for outside joist

Edge even with end of ledger

Upper-level site

Lower-level site

1 Use a plumb bob or carpenter's level to reference down from the edge of the ledger to the slab. (Note that the shims are 1½ inches longer than the ledger to accommodate the thickness of the outside joist.) To draw a line exactly perpendicular to the house, lay a straight board on the slab, and use the 3–4–5 method (*page 36*) to set it perpendicular to the foundation. Draw a line on the slab along the edge of the board. This line indicates the edge of an outside joist for the lower level.

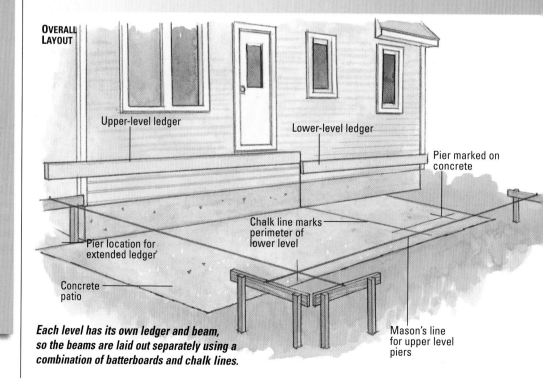

OVERALL LAYOUT

Upper-level ledger

Lower-level ledger

Pier marked on concrete

Pier location for extended ledger

Chalk line marks perimeter of lower level

Concrete patio

Mason's line for upper level piers

Each level has its own ledger and beam, so the beams are laid out separately using a combination of batterboards and chalk lines.

Center of pier

Outside of joist

2 Snap chalk lines on the slab indicating the outside of the joists. Measure from those lines to locate the footings. Check and recheck your work.

Plumb from post location marked on ledger

Mason's line

3 Where the ledger runs past the house, reference down with a carpenter's level or a plumb line and use batterboards and mason's line to find the footing locations.

Jackhammer

4 Rent a jackhammer to cut holes in the concrete slab to accommodate footings. Make the holes a few inches wider than the tube forms.

WHAT IF ...
A vent must go through the ledger?

If a vent must run through the ledger, remove the vent cap and its tailpiece. If the vent does not fall between joists, you may need to frame out to make room for the vent (see *page 69*). Carefully measure for the center of the hole and use a hole saw to cut the hole. You may need to attach a longer tailpiece to the vent cap before replacing it. **Hole saws can bind and buck. Practice with this tool before cutting the ledger board.**

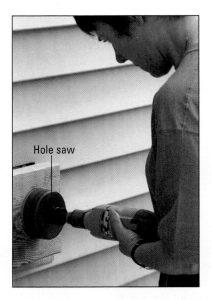

Hole saw

REFRESHER COURSE
Fastening a ledger

Attach the ledger with a pair of lag screws about every 16 inches. The screws must be long enough to dig through the entire thickness of the framing member behind the siding *(page 61)*. Place the screws where they will not get in the way of joists.

Upper-level outside joist goes here

Ledger for lower level

Lower-level outside joist goes here

INSTALLING THE BEAMS

Form and pour the footings with J-bolts and allow the concrete to cure for 48 hours. Install post anchors and install posts that are a foot or so taller than they need to be (see *pages 42–43*). Plumb the posts using a post level *(page 42)* and brace the posts firmly with 1×4s so they won't move when they get jostled during construction of the beams.

Building a two-part beam

Some inspectors prefer an on-top beam made of two 2×s fastened together *(pages 44 and 66)* because the resulting beam is actually stronger than the sum of the two parts. Others prefer the two-part beam shown on these pages, because attaching to the sides of the posts adds stability. Most inspectors will accept either type of beam. Confirm local requirements.

1 Use a mason's line and two blocks of 1× to check if the ledger is straight. If it has waves of 1 inch or less, install the outside joists and header first, then add the inside joists. If the ledger has major waves, using that technique will result in a wavy header; instead follow the steps on *pages 91–93*.

2 Rest one end of a straight board on the ledger and have a helper check for level as you mark an outside post. From this mark measure down the width of the joists to mark the top of the beam. Repeat for the other outside post.

BEAM AND LEDGER OVERVIEW

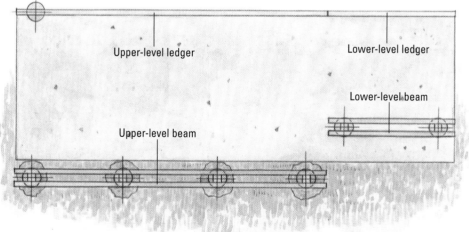

Four piers sunk into the yard support the beam for the upper level, while two piers cut into the slab support the beam for the lower level.

3 Measure down the width of the beam lumber and attach a temporary brace to each outside post to support the beam pieces as you work.

4 Cut two beam pieces to length and mark them for post locations (see below). Put a beam piece on the temporary brace with its crown side up and adjust it until it is level. Temporarily fasten it at the end opposite the brace with a 3-inch screw. Install the second member on the other side of the post. **Double-check that the beam is at the correct height to support the joists.**

STANLEY PRO TIP: **Mark for post locations**

To avoid awkward measuring as you install the beams, clamp them together and mark the location of each post. Strike a line with a square and mark an X to indicate the location of the posts. Let the end of the beam run long a few inches. It can be trimmed once you are satisfied with the joist locations.

Decorative beam cuts

If the end of a beam will be visible, cut a 45-degree angle in the bottom of each piece for a cleaner look. Before making the cut, make sure the crown side is facing up.

Installing the beams (continued)

Carriage bolt

Socket wrench

5 Clamp the beam members to draw them tightly against the post. Attach the second piece in the same way as the first. Using an extended drill bit, drill two holes through the beam pieces and the post for the carriage bolts.

Extended bit

6 Tap 7-inch carriage bolts through the holes. Make sure the bolt heads face the outside of the deck; they have a more finished look than the nuts.

7 Slip a washer and turn a nut onto each bolt. Tighten the nut with a ratchet wrench. It's a good idea to use a deep socket or an extension on the wrench to avoid banging your knuckles on the beam.

STANLEY PRO TIP: **Cutting the post**

Reciprocating saw

With a reciprocating saw. Once the beam is installed, cut the post flush with the tops of the beam pieces. (If the post sticks up even a little the decking will be uneven.) One method is to use a reciprocating saw. Don't worry if you gouge the pieces, it will be covered by decking.

Or with a circular saw... Adjust the blade on a circular saw for as deep a cut as possible and cut two sides of the post. Retract the blade guard and use the top of a beam piece as a guide for the blade.

...and handsaw. Finish the cut with a hand saw. If part of the post is a little too high, use a belt sander or file to level it off.

INSTALLING JOISTS

Use the joist installation method shown on these pages if the ledger is not straight (see Step 1, *page 88,* to check ledger). In this method, you attach all the joists to the ledger and cut them to length afterward.

Before attaching a joist to the ledger, check that the end is square and that there are no splits or cracks. If you find a flaw, cut off about an inch or turn the board around and install the other end (if it is square and unflawed) onto the ledger. Make sure each joist is installed with its crown facing up.

If the ledger is straight, install the outside joists and header first and check them for square. Cut all the inside joists to the same length and install them with joist hangers *(pages 48–49)*.

Check with your local building department whether codes require hanger nails or screws *(page 48)*.

PRESTART CHECKLIST

☐ **TIME**
With a helper, about 4 to 5 hours to install 20 joists and a header

☐ **TOOLS**
Tape measure, hammer, drill, circular saw, chalk line, layout square

☐ **SKILLS**
Measuring and cutting boards, driving screws or nails and attaching joist hangers

☐ **PREP**
Install the ledger and the beam, check the ledger for straightness, and draw layout lines on the ledger *(page 60)*

☐ **MATERIALS**
Joists, joist hangers, screws or nails

1 Screw a temporary cleat to the top of a joist, extending outward about an inch. Rest the cleat on the ledger. Align the joist with the layout lines, install a joist hanger on the ledger, and fasten the joist to the hanger.

2 Check that the outside joists are square to the ledger. Transfer the layout lines on the ledger to a long 1×4. At the other end of the joists, temporarily attach the 1×4 to the joists so they are spaced correctly.

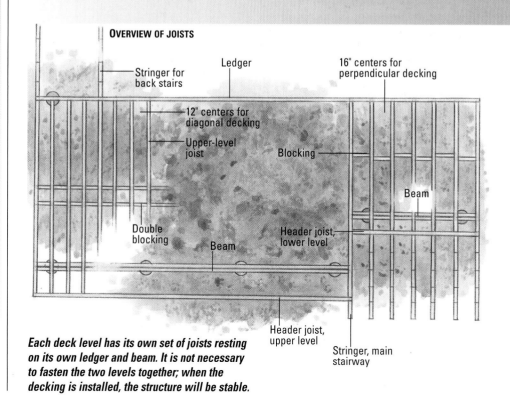

OVERVIEW OF JOISTS

Stringer for back stairs

Ledger

16" centers for perpendicular decking

12" centers for diagonal decking

Upper-level joist

Blocking

Beam

Double blocking

Beam

Header joist, lower level

Header joist, upper level

Stringer, main stairway

Each deck level has its own set of joists resting on its own ledger and beam. It is not necessary to fasten the two levels together; when the decking is installed, the structure will be stable.

Installing joists (continued)

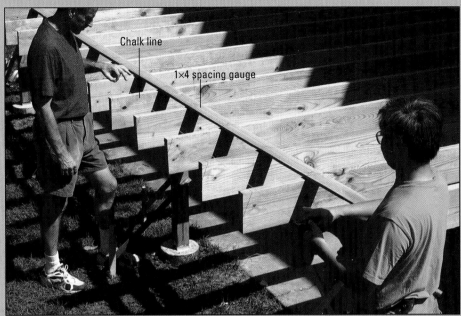

3 Once all the joists are installed and evenly spaced, measure out from the house and mark the top of both end joists for cutting. Keep in mind that the thickness of the header joist will add 1½ inches to the length of the framing, and that the decking will overhang the framing by another 1½ inches. Stretch a chalk line from mark to mark and snap it. Check that there is a clear line on top of every joist.

Use a layout square to mark the cut line on the side of every joist (see Step 7, *page 93*). **Be sure each cut line meets the on-top chalk line precisely.**

4 Cut each joist with a circular saw. Cutting a vertical line is a bit tricky, so practice on some scrap pieces first. You may cut freehand or with a layout square or scrap of 1× clamped on as a guide. Cutting down lets the weight of the saw do some of the work; cut upward if it seems more comfortable.

STANLEY PRO TIP

Use a header support

It's difficult to hold a header precisely in place while driving screws or nails. Screw a scrap piece of wood to the underside of the outside joists to support the header as you work.

5 Cut the header to length—usually 3 inches longer than the ledger. With a helper, hold it up against the joists and drive 3-inch screws or 16-penny galvanized nails to attach it to an end joist. Attach to the other joists in the same way. **Make sure the top of the header is flush with the top of the joists.**

Mark line midway between the ledger and the beam.

6 To mark for the position of blocking pieces, snap a chalk line across the top of the joists. Blocking is usually installed midway between the ledger and the beam.

7 At each chalk line, draw a square line down both sides of the joist. Cut blocking pieces to fit between the joists. They should be 1½ inches shorter than the layout spacing. For instance, if joists are 16 inches on center, cut 14½-inch-long pieces. For 12-inch centers use 10½-inch blocking pieces.

8 Unless you have a special reason to line the blocking pieces in a straight row (see below left), install the blocking in staggered fashion for ease of fastening. Drive two or three screws or nails through the side of each joist.

WHAT IF ...
Blocking pieces double as nailers?

Sometimes blocking is needed to provide a nailing surface for the decking. This deck's design calls for a center decking strip with angled pieces that butt against it. Two straight rows of blocking, 6½ inches apart, are needed to support the ends of the angled decking pieces. When using blocking to support decking, take special care that the top of the blocking is perfectly flush with the top of the joists; if blocking is even ⅛ inch lower or higher than a nearby joist, the decking surface will be uneven.

Blocking

Keep blocking flush with joists.

STANLEY PRO TIP

Measure blocking

Every few blocking pieces, check that the joists are correctly spaced. You may need to cut a blocking piece a little short or long to bring the joists back into alignment.

DECKING WITH A CENTER STRIP

If you attempt to install angled decking boards that meet at their miter cuts, expect a struggle. Decking boards may vary in width by as much as ¼ inch, making it very difficult to maintain perfect joints. If the spacing between boards varies or one board bows slightly, the joint will gap. The project is much more manageable if you install a center strip and butt the miter-cut boards against it.

This pattern has another advantage: Because you end up with two relatively narrow sections of decking, most of the boards that run between the house and the center strip are exactly the same size. The boards that run from the center strip to the outside of the deck can be miter-cut on one end only; let the other end run wild, so you can finish with a chalk line cut.

PRESTART CHECKLIST

☐ **TIME**
About 8 hours to cut and install angled decking with a center strip for a 300-square-foot deck

☐ **TOOLS**
Tape measure, hammer, drill, circular saw, layout square, power miter saw, chalk line

☐ **SKILLS**
Making consistently accurate 45-degree miter cuts, fastening with screws or nails

☐ **PREP**
Install framing with two parallel rows of blocking (page 93)

☐ **MATERIALS**
Decking boards, nails or screws

¼-inch plywood spacer

Center strip

1 Temporarily attach a strip of ¼-inch plywood against the house to act as a spacer. Choose a particularly straight decking board to use as the center strip. Position it midway between the rows of blocking and measure at various points to make sure it is exactly parallel to the house. (If the deck section between the strip and the header is slightly narrower or wider than the section between the strip and the house, that will not be noticeable.) Double-check that the board is straight, and fasten it with two screws or nails driven into each joist.

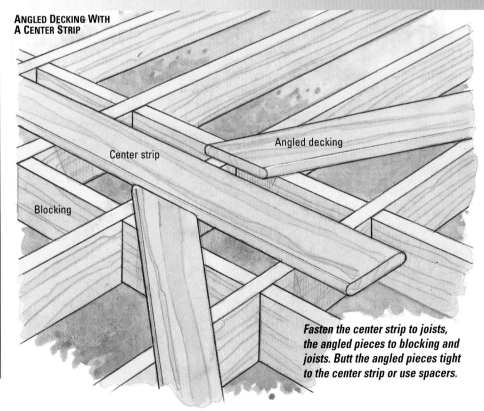

ANGLED DECKING WITH A CENTER STRIP

Angled decking

Center strip

Blocking

Fasten the center strip to joists, the angled pieces to blocking and joists. Butt the angled pieces tight to the center strip or use spacers.

Distances are equal when board is at 45 degrees.

2 Practice with a power miter saw (shown above) or circular saw until you are sure you can make precise 45-degree cuts in all the decking boards. Set up the work site for comfort and ease, so that making these cuts is routine.

3 Miter-cut the end of one board and hold it in position on the deck with one end resting on the center strip. Measure from the corner of the resulting triangle in two directions, as shown above. When the measurements are equal, the board is at 45 degrees to the house. There should be a space of about ⅛ inch between the center strip and decking. Subtract the ⅛ inch when marking the boards or just cut to the "good" side of the mark instead of the waste side. The saw blade will remove about ⅛ inch.

Cut with circular saw

With practice and a professional-quality circular saw, you can make accurate 45-degree miter cuts with little trouble. Test your skills on scrap pieces of wood and don't try cutting actual decking boards until you are sure of your skills. First, try holding a layout square with one hand while cutting with the other hand. If you find that the blade guard refuses to retract, try clamping the square as shown at right so you can retract the guard as you work.

Make a 45-degree cutting jig

A jig like this makes it possible to cut accurate 45-degree miters with a circular saw. Cut off the corner of a piece of plywood so that you have an equilateral triangle with each side of the triangle about 11 inches long. Drive three screws to fasten the cut side of the triangle to a piece of 1×. Use clamps to help hold the jig firmly on the board to be cut.

Decking with a center strip *(continued)*

4 Place the decking board in position with one end pressed against the plywood spacer at the house and the other end against the center strip. Use nails to space the miter-cut piece slightly away from the center strip. Measure again to see that the board is at a 45-degree angle to the house (Step 3, *page 95*). Sight down the length of the board to see that it is straight. Fasten it with as many nails or screws as needed to keep the board straight.

Spacer nail

5 For boards on the other side of the center strip, miter cut one end only. Use a layout square to make sure that the first board on this side is directly across from a board on the house side. Check that the board is straight and fasten it with as many fasteners as needed to keep it straight.

Use a layout square to align opposing boards.

REFRESHER COURSE
Check the boards

Before purchasing decking, make a scale drawing to plan the most efficient use of available lengths *(page 50)*. Make a list of the lengths needed, adding 10 or 15 percent for waste and rejects. You can cut back that margin if you handpick the decking, but allow at least 5 percent for mistakes and defects that you might miss. If you handpick the boards, look for defects *(page 16)* such as crooks, twists, splits, loose knots, wane, and cupping. Confirm that at least one side is smooth and defect-free enough. On the site, store the decking flat, away from moisture—in a sheltered area if possible.

HERRINGBONE DECKING

2×4 nailer

Joist

2×4 nailer

To install herringbone decking, position joints that are symmetrically spaced on the deck. At each joint, triple the width of the joist by fastening a 2×4 cleat on either side. Install full-length pieces first, then the shorter pieces.

Piece that butts against house

Boards run wild

Chalk line

Guide board

6 Once some full-length pieces are installed, measure for the shorter pieces on the house side; these must be miter-cut on both ends. For each piece, cut one end at a 45-degree miter. Place the board in the position where it will go, with one end pressed against the plywood spacer and nails used as spacers along its length. Mark the board for the miter cut on the other end.

7 Let the boards on the other side run wild. Once all the boards are installed with as many fasteners as needed to keep them straight, snap a chalk line 1½ inches out from the header joist and cut along the line. Tack a long, straight board as a guide to ensure a straight cut. Once the decking is trimmed, strike a chalk line at each joist and drive the rest of the fasteners *(page 72)*. Drill pilot holes before adding fasteners near the ends of boards *(page 71)*.

OTHER DECKING PATTERNS

A V-shape design (below right) calls for a doubled joist in the center of the framing. Work carefully to maintain consistent, tight joints.

Double joist

A parquet design (above left) is easy to build— the framing is not complicated and all the decking boards are the same length.

WHAT IF...
You need to eliminate small pieces on a step?

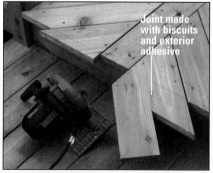

Joint made with biscuits and exterior adhesive

Despite the best-laid plans, you may end up with an awkward piece at the wrong spot— in this case, on a step. If varying the spacing to end up with a whole piece *(page 52)* doesn't work, consider making a large piece of decking using a biscuit joiner and exterior adhesive. Rip cut the decking for a smooth joint.

BUILDING DEEP AND WIDE STAIRS

Stair treads that are 14 inches wide make a graceful transition to the lawn and provide comfortable places for people to sit and relax.

For complete steps on calculating and building a stairway, see *pages 73–77.* Stairs with 14-inch runs (tread widths) should have rises of between 5½ and 6½ inches.

The wider the treads the more total run the stringers have to span. When you notch stringers, you weaken them. After the notches are cut out of these 2×12 stringers, about 5½ inches of uncut width is left for strength—in other words, the stringers are as strong as 2×6s. These stringers have to span a distance of about 9 feet, which is close to the limit for a 2×6 joist (see the chart, *page 22).* So 2×4 cleats were added for extra strength (Step 7).

PRESTART CHECKLIST

☐ **TIME**
Most of a day to install a set of stairs like those shown

☐ **TOOLS**
Tape measure, circular saw, handsaw, hammer, drill, framing square

☐ **SKILLS**
Calculating rise and run for a stairway, measuring and cutting with a circular saw, fastening with nails or screws

☐ **PREP**
Review *pages 73–77* of this book

☐ **MATERIALS**
2×12 for stringers, pavers, sand, and edging for the landing pad surface, decking for the treads, 2×4 toe kick, lag screws with masonry shields

1 Install a cross brace directly beneath the joist to provide adequate surface for attaching the stringers. Connect the brace firmly to posts or the beam, so it is just as strong as the joist above it.

Framing square — Stair gauge set to unit rise — Stair gauge set to unit run

2 Calculate rise and run and mark a stringer using a framing square. Cut the top and bottom of the stringer and hold it in position to determine the location and height of the landing pad *(page 74).*

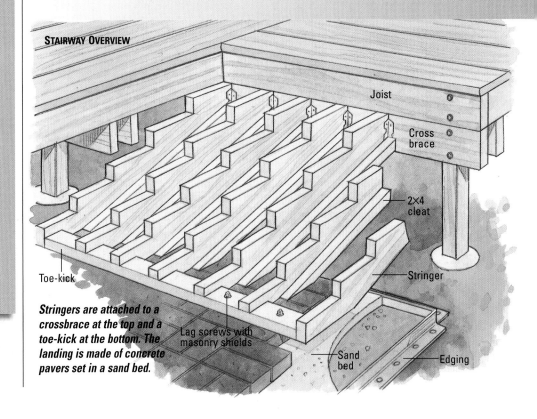

STAIRWAY OVERVIEW

Joist — Cross brace — 2×4 cleat — Stringer — Toe-kick — Lag screws with masonry shields — Sand bed — Edging

Stringers are attached to a crossbrace at the top and a toe-kick at the bottom. The landing is made of concrete pavers set in a sand bed.

3 To construct a paver landing pad, excavate the site. Install several inches of crushed limestone and tamp it firm. Install edging and check that the corners are square.

4 Use a straight board to spread 1 or 2 inches of sand over the limestone to form a level surface that is one paver's thickness lower than the finished height of the pad.

5 Set the pavers on top of the sand. If you need to cut any pavers, use a rented masonry saw. You may be able to avoid cutting pavers by adjusting the position of the edging. When the pavers are laid, sweep extra-fine sand into the joints; tamp firm and repeat.

6 Cut the stringers (pages 74–75). Notch the inside stringers for the toe-kick. Attach the stringers at the top to the crossbrace. Anchor the toe kick to the pad using lag screws and masonry anchors.

7 Attach the stringers to the toe-kick by toe-fastening with 3-inch deck screws. To add extra strength, attach a 2×4 cleat to the side of each stringer. For each step, install the riser board first, then the tread boards. Clamp a scrap 2×4 to the side of an outside stringer to help maintain a consistent 1½-inch overhang. For treads, you can use two full-width decking boards and one board rip-cut to a narrower width.

ADDING AN UPGRADED RAILING

For a small amount of time and money, you can build a railing that is distinctive and handsome. This railing design is a variation on the one shown on *pages 80–83*; see those pages for complete instructions on planning and assembling a basic railing.

None of the steps used in building this railing require special woodworking tools or skills. All the pieces can be cut with a circular saw, though a power miter saw or a radial-arm saw will make the job easier. The pieces are attached with screws or nails; fancy joints are not needed.

The post is made of 2×4s and 1×4s that in combination are much less likely to develop cracks than a standard 4×4 post. A built-up post also lends a handcrafted appearance to the deck.

Consult with local building codes to determine the required overall height of the railing, as well as how far apart the balusters must be.

PRESTART CHECKLIST

☐ **TIME**
   Working with a helper, a day to construct about 60 running feet of railing

☐ **TOOLS**
   Tape measure, hammer, drill, circular saw, layout square, post level, ratchet and socket

☐ **SKILLS**
   Measuring and cutting boards, laying out for consistently spaced balusters, fastening with nails or screws

☐ **PREP**
   Determine post locations and notch the decking to accommodate *(page 81)*

☐ **MATERIALS**
   2×4, 1×4 for posts; 2×4 for top, bottom rails; 2×6 or ⁵⁄₄ decking for rail cap; 4-inch lag screws; 2- or 3-inch deck screws or nails; angle brackets

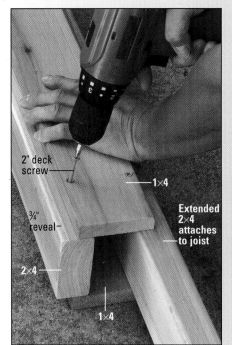

1 To make a regular post, cut two 1×4s and one 2×4 to the height of the railing, minus the thickness of the rail cap. Cut another 2×4 to the same length, plus the combined width of the outside joist and the decking's thickness. Fasten by drilling pilot holes and driving screws or nails.

2 A corner post is made with three 2×4s and one 1×4. Use a scrap of 1×4 as a guide for the ¾-inch reveal along the edges of all the boards. Join 2×4s with 3-inch deck screws.

RAILING OVERVIEW

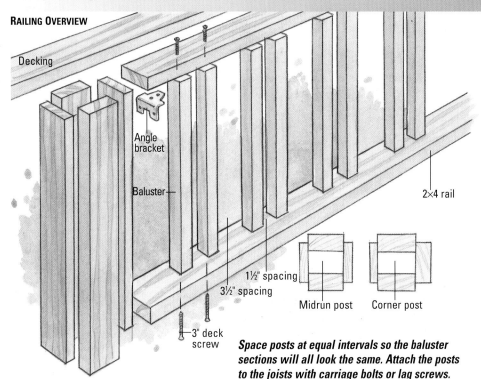

Space posts at equal intervals so the baluster sections will all look the same. Attach the posts to the joists with carriage bolts or lag screws.

3 For each post, notch the decking so the longer 2×4 can attach tight to the joist. Position the post with the short boards resting on top of the decking. Hold the post plumb, drive pilot holes, and attach with lag screws or carriage bolts *(page 81)*.

4 Measure the distance between the posts and cut two 2×4 rails to fit. Mark on the rails for balusters that are evenly spaced; you may choose a paired pattern as shown—an alternating spacing of 1½ inches and 3½ inches. Set the rails on a flat surface, and lay two pieces of decking as spacers next to them so that the 2×2 balusters will be centered within the width of the rail. Attach the balusters to the rails with one screw or nail driven into each joint.

5 Set some 2×4 scraps on the deck to temporarily hold the baluster section up so its top is flush with the top of the posts. Slip the baluster section into place and clamp it. Drill angled pilot holes and drive nails or screws as shown.

6 Reinforce the top rails with angle brackets. Attach a rail cap to the top of the railing, as shown on *page 83*. One advantage of this approach is that the whole railing section can be removed for future maintenance—especially helpful if you choose to paint it.

BUILDING A PERGOLA

This structure may look complicated, but taken step-by-step it is easy to build. The most difficult part is working above your head, so have a pair of stable stepladders on hand and enlist a reliable helper.

Because only one row of posts is used in this design, the pergola can be no wider than 6 feet. If you want a larger amount of shade, install at least two rows of posts with beams. Use 2×6s for beams and rafters that span up to 8 feet, and 2×8s for beams or rafters with spans of up to 11 feet.

The detailing of the pergola can be changed easily to suit your taste. Choose a simple or ornate design for the ends of the beams and rafters (see box on opposite page). Position the top pieces closer for more shade, farther apart for less shade.

PRESTART CHECKLIST

☐ **TIME**
Working with a helper, most of a day to build a three-tiered overhead with a lattice panel

☐ **TOOLS**
Tape measure, hammer, drill, circular saw, post level, carpenter's level, layout square, ratchet and socket, sandpaper

☐ **SKILLS**
Measuring and cutting boards, checking posts for plumb, fastening while working on a ladder

☐ **PREP**
Notch the decking so that posts can go tight up against the outside joist

☐ **MATERIALS**
4×4 posts, 2×6 rafters, 2×8 beams, 1×2 for top pieces; lattice, 2×4 and 2×2 frame for lattice; hurricane ties; 1½", 3" screws

6" carriage bolt

Post anchor

1 Cut posts to the desired height, and anchor them so they have lateral strength. In this case, posts are bolted to a joist and attached to a post anchor on a concrete patio. If you need to set posts in a posthole (page 43), cut them to height after the concrete has set.

Mark for positioning rafters

Overhang mark

2 Cut the rafters to the same length, and mark them for the distance they will overhang. Clamp them together with their crowns facing up; lay out and mark them for the installation of top pieces.

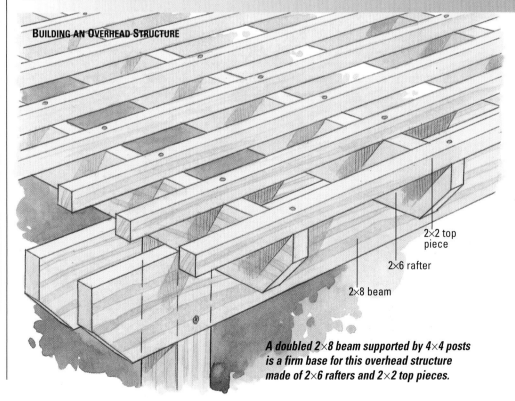

BUILDING AN OVERHEAD STRUCTURE

2×2 top piece

2×6 rafter

2×8 beam

A doubled 2×8 beam supported by 4×4 posts is a firm base for this overhead structure made of 2×6 rafters and 2×2 top pieces.

3 Cut two 2×8 beams to the same length. Hold them together with their crowns facing up, and lay out on their tops for rafters that are evenly spaced. To hold the rafters, install hurricane ties on one beam where they will be least visible. Attach the beams to the posts with 3-inch deck screws.

4 Center each rafter on the beams, using the overhang mark made in Step 2. Attach each rafter with a hurricane tie on one beam and by toe-fastening screws into the other beam.

Cut 2×2 top pieces to length. Mark for a 6-inch overhang at each end. Attach the top pieces to the rafters with 3-inch screws or nails. Sand any rough edges with medium-grit sandpaper.

WHAT IF...
You want an ornamental touch?

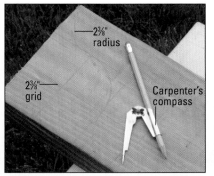

Experiment with a compass to come up with two or three curves as shown. If you wish to mimic an element of your house, you may be able to trace the design on a piece of cardboard and then transfer the design to the board. Once you have cut one board, use it as a template for marking the others.

5 Cut 2×4s to span from post to post, and install them by drilling angled pilot holes and driving screws or nails. To provide a nailing surface for the lattice, attach a 2×2 nailer flush with the inside edges of the 2×4s and the 4×4 post.

6 Cut a lattice panel to fit inside the frame, and attach it to the nailers with nails or screws. Cut pieces of 2×2 and install them tightly to the lattice so that the lattice is sandwiched between two pieces of 2×2.

ADDING SKIRTING

If a deck is raised high enough that you can see under it, you may want to cover the framing and footings with skirting.

Unless you live in a dry climate, make sure the skirt provides enough ventilation that the area underneath can dry out between rainfalls. If you install skirting made of solid 1×s instead of lattice, leave at least ½-inch spaces between the boards. The vinyl lattice shown here is ideal—it won't rot and it requires no painting.

Making it strong enough

If the skirt will be less than 2 feet high and in a low-traffic area, attach it to the joist leaving its bottom edge unsupported. For a skirt that can withstand bumps from a lawn mower or errant soccer ball, frame along the bottom: Tie the horizontal piece at the bottom to the posts under the deck, keeping it at least ¾ inch above grade. Use only pressure-treated lumber.

If you want to use the space under a deck for storage, frame one of the skirt sections with 2×4 or 1×4. For occasional access, attach the section with screws that can be removed. If you need access often, install hinges and a latch.

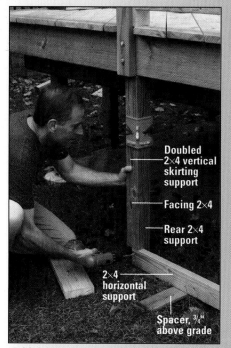

1 Make a vertical support by cutting one 2×4 so it reaches from behind the joist down to ¾ inch above grade. Cut a facing 2×4 to extend from the bottom of the joist to the top of the horizontal support. Plumb the support; attach the pieces with 3-inch screws. Install the horizontal pieces.

2 Attach outriggers to the horizontal framing members. Notch each outrigger so it fits over the horizontal 2×4. Use a mason's line to check that the horizontal 2×4 is straight. Install all the outriggers with two 3-inch screws or nails in each joint and into the posts.

PRESTART CHECKLIST

☐ **TIME**
About a day to frame and install about 40 feet of lattice skirting

☐ **TOOLS**
Tape measure, post level, drill, hammer, circular saw, handsaw, square, string

☐ **SKILLS**
Improvising a framing plan, cutting boards, fastening with screws or nails

☐ **PREP**
Choose a skirt material that suits your needs. Estimate materials for framing.

☐ **MATERIALS**
2×4 for framing; lattice panels or other skirt material; 1×2 or 1×4 for trim; ⅞-inch roofing nails; 2- or 3-inch deck screws or nails

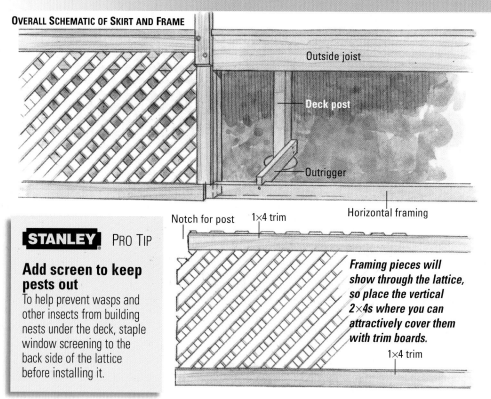

OVERALL SCHEMATIC OF SKIRT AND FRAME

STANLEY PRO TIP

Add screen to keep pests out

To help prevent wasps and other insects from building nests under the deck, staple window screening to the back side of the lattice before installing it.

Framing pieces will show through the lattice, so place the vertical 2×4s where you can attractively cover them with trim boards.

1× spacer to
hold 2×4 above
grade ¾ inch

3 At an outside corner, attach two outriggers to hold the horizontal 2×4s firmly. Cut the end of a horizontal piece with a handsaw. The 1×4 trim will overlap at the corner. If the horizontal 2×4 follows the grade, decide whether or not the lattice and trim should as well. For appearance's sake, it may be best to level the lattice and trim even if some of the horizontal 2×4 will show. (Use plantings to disguise it.)

4 Lay the lattice on scrap pieces of lumber so you have a stable edge for cutting. Mark the lattice for cutting using a chalk line or a framing square and pencil (a drywall-type T-square is even better if you have one). Cut the lines with a circular saw, setting the blade so it extends ¼ inch beyond the lattice.

5 Notch the lattice to fit tightly along the sides of the railing posts. All other lattice edges will be covered by 1×4 trim, so cut the lattice about ¼ inch short for easy installation. Buy ⅞-inch galvanized roofing nails to fasten the lattice in place. Use just enough nails to keep the lattice from sagging—the 1×4 trim will actually support it.

1×4 trim fastened
to header joist

Trim fastened
to skirt frame

Trim fastened
to skirt post

6 Install the trim of your choice. In this example, 1×4 is used—1×2 would work as well. Start by installing the horizontal trim, fastening it into the bottom 2×4 frame and the outside joist with two 2-inch fasteners every 18 inches. Beneath the deck posts, add trim to cover the vertical skirt frame. Finally add trim under the decking. Just a portion of the joist will show through the lattice.

FINISHING & REPAIRING

A deck is usually in an exposed location, where it is subject to the ravages of the elements. Many older decks are built of nontreated or poorly treated lumber, making them easy targets for rot.

Exposure to the sun causes untreated wood to turn gray. In the case of redwood, this is an attractive silver color. If the wood is pressure-treated, the color is less attractive. Either way, the gray can be removed by washing with a deck cleaner.

Overexposure to the sun dries out the wood, opening the grain and turning tiny cracks into major splits. Sun-dried boards will curl and twist if they are not securely fastened every 16 inches or so.

If moisture is allowed to sit on wood surfaces for long periods, wet rot can be the result. Wet rot usually starts in crevices and joints where water collects and is slow to dry out. If a board is substantially rotted, it should be replaced. *Pages 108–113* show how to diagnose rot and shore up or replace damaged boards.

Moisture may also lead to black, slimy mildew. Fortunately, you can quickly treat mildew by washing the affected area.

Once you've finished building a deck—or when it's time to refinish your old deck—protect your investment by applying sealer or stain or both. Check with a lumber supplier to find out which product works best for your wood and in your area; *pages 114–115* will help you choose.

Proper care, use of stain or sealer, and simple repairs keep a deck looking good for many years.

CHAPTER PREVIEW

Diagnosing deck problems
page 108

Repairing decking
page 110

Repairing framing
page 112

Applying a finish
page 114

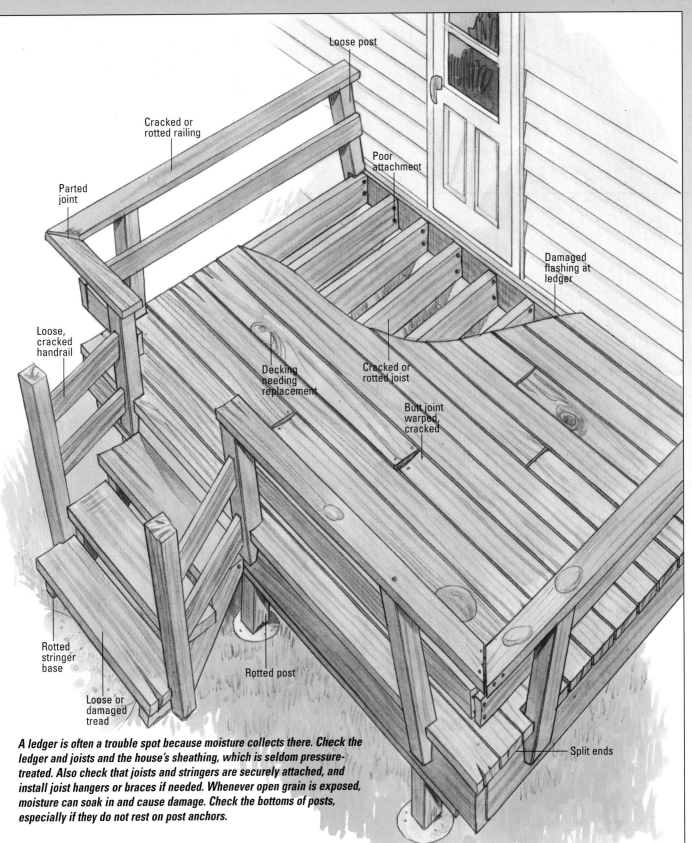

Loose post

Cracked or
rotted railing

Parted
joint

Poor
attachment

Damaged
flashing at
ledger

Loose,
cracked
handrail

Decking
needing
replacement

Cracked or
rotted joist

Butt joint
warped,
cracked

Rotted
stringer
base

Rotted post

Loose or
damaged
tread

Split ends

*A ledger is often a trouble spot because moisture collects there. Check the
ledger and joists and the house's sheathing, which is seldom pressure-
treated. Also check that joists and stringers are securely attached, and
install joist hangers or braces if needed. Whenever open grain is exposed,
moisture can soak in and cause damage. Check the bottoms of posts,
especially if they do not rest on post anchors.*

DIAGNOSING DECK PROBLEMS

If a deck is in serious trouble, you can often feel it before you see it. Some boards or sections feel spongy when you walk on them. Railings feel wobbly.

Don't wait for these symptoms of wood rot to manifest themselves before you take action. A quick tour of your deck, screwdriver and flashlight in hand, enables you to spot trouble before it takes its toll.

If possible, find out the type of lumber used in your deck *(pages 14–15)*. If the boards are untreated fir, pine, or hemlock, apply generous coats of sealer even if you find no symptoms yet; these woods can develop rot in a matter of months.

Probe the boards with a screwdriver. If it sinks in easily, rot is present. Chances are if one board is rotted, the boards attached to it are rotted as well. If the rot is shallow, clean the area, let it dry, and apply plenty of sealer. You may want to add a cleat for extra strength *(page 110)*. Take steps to ensure that the spot will not remain wet after a rainfall. If the rot is deeper than an inch or so, the board should be replaced.

PRESTART CHECKLIST

☐ **TIME**
About an hour to make a fairly thorough inspection of a medium-size deck

☐ **TOOLS**
Screwdriver, flashlight, putty knife

☐ **SKILLS**
Attention to detail

☐ **PREP**
Remove skirting, if any, so you can get at the underside of the deck

☐ **MATERIALS**
None needed

Crevice between decking and ledger

Check the ledger first. Stick a screwdriver into the top and side of the ledger. (Don't jab at any metal flashing; you could poke a hole in it.) If the wood feels spongy, rot is present. This rot may also be present on the underside of decking boards or in the house's sheathing.

Check each post where it abuts decking, where it attaches to a joist, at its top, and at its bottom. Poke with a screwdriver to find any areas of rot.

Grasp posts or railings and give a good shake; if the railing feels loose, the situation could be dangerous. Check for rot, but the problem may be loose fasteners. Sometimes bad design is the culprit—there may not be enough fastening surface for the post.

Rail caps are often the most exposed members of a deck. Check all the parts of a railing for looseness and refasten as needed by drilling pilot holes and driving screws or nails. Balusters are often attached with only one fastener at either end, so some may come loose in time.

For decking that is generally cracked and split, try sanding the surface, then applying several coats of sealer. If decking boards are cracked at the ends, consider making a chalk-line cut *(page 72)* as long as the decking overhangs the joist sufficiently. Apply sealer to the cut ends.

If dirt or leaves collect between decking boards or in other crevices, moisture will remain for weeks at a time. This almost certainly will lead to rot unless the wood is well treated. Keep a deck clean to forestall rot. Try to clean between decking on an annual basis.

View from below: Put on old clothes, grab a flashlight and screwdriver, and venture below the deck. Check the undersides of decking boards, all around the ledger, posts, stringers, and treads, and in any other joints and crevices.

STANLEY PRO TIP: **Enough sealant?**

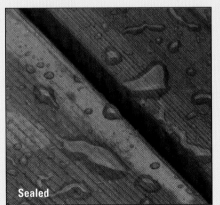

Is your deck sealed properly? In some cases, the answer is obvious. Old wood with a dried-out look clearly needs a stiff dose of sealer. But boards that look OK may also be in danger of drying out. So do a quick test once or twice a year. Sprinkle a little water onto the surface.

If the water beads up and does not soak in within two minutes, the board is sealed well enough. If water soaks in within two minutes, it's time to apply sealer *(pages 114–115)*.

Got bugs?

If termites, carpenter ants, or other wood-boring insects are a problem in your area, your deck may be on their menu. Pressure-treated lumber rated at ".40 CCA" or labeled "ground contact" *(page 14)* is probably safe, but nontreated wood, including redwood and cedar, is at risk.

A "primary infestation" of wood-boring insects means that the colony (with its queen) lives in the ground, where it can find moisture, and makes daily forays to find wood. A "secondary infestation" occurs when the wood itself provides enough moisture that the pests can encamp right inside a board.

These creatures don't like sunlight, so they tunnel inside boards where you can't see them. That means once you see the damage, it's probably too late to save the board. If you see tunnels running inside a board, usually following a grain, you've got bugs. Consult with a professional exterminator.

REPAIRING DECKING

It's not unusual for several decking boards to be damaged on a deck that's otherwise in good condition. Replacing a board or two is not difficult. New boards, if they are of the same type as the old ones, may blend in color with the old boards after a year or two. If you clean and refinish the entire deck, the new boards typically will blend in right away.

To refasten boards, it may help to use deck screws that are 3½ or 4 inches long.

Opening the gaps
Decking boards should have gaps between them, about ⅛ inch wide, so that water can seep through and dry out after a rainfall. If a gap is filled with debris, clean it out with a stiff broom. If that doesn't work, use a putty knife. If cleaning isn't enough, widen a gap by cutting with a circular saw.

PRESTART CHECKLIST

☐ **TIME**
An hour or two for most deck repairs

☐ **TOOLS**
Hammer, drill, flat pry bar, taping knife, cat's paw, circular saw, saber saw or reciprocating saw

☐ **SKILLS**
Making straight cuts in boards that are fastened, fastening with nails or screws

☐ **PREP**
Inspect the deck for damage to framing and plan to make additional repairs, if needed

☐ **MATERIALS**
Decking boards, nails or screws

A. Cutting to replace part of a board

1 If only part of a long board is damaged and you don't want to replace the entire board, replace a section at least three joists long. Use a saber saw to cut on the waste side of the joist. Begin the cut between the boards and curve into a perpendicular cut; reverse cut to finish.

2 Install a 2×4 cleat to provide a fastening surface for the new board. Fasten the new board in place with 2½-inch deck screws. Allow the new board to run past the end of the deck and cut it to length after the board is fastened.

WHAT IF...
Decking is warped upward?

Draw it down with a screw...
Warped boards can often be tamed with a stronger fastener. If you don't mind the appearance of an extra fastener head, drill a pilot hole and drive a screw next to the existing fasteners. For a neater look, remove the old fasteners and drive screws that are at least 1 inch longer than the old fasteners.

Or hold it with an angle-driven screw
Force the warped board down and drill a pilot hole at an angle. Drive the fastener.

If a board does not lie down all the way after refastening, wait a week for it to become partially flattened and try driving the fastener (or an even longer one) again.

B. Removing decking

1 If a nail head is partially popped up, pry it out using a flat pry bar. If the decking is soft wood (cedar or redwood is softer than pressure-treated lumber), protect the wood with a taping knife placed under the pry bar (see Step 3).

2 If you will be throwing out the board anyway, use a cat's paw to dig in under the nailhead and pry the nail partway out. Finish prying with the claw of a hammer.

3 To remove a board without damaging a neighboring piece, start at the end where the board overhangs the deck. If that is not possible, use a flat pry bar and a taping knife to shoehorn the damaged board out.

STANLEY PRO TIP: **Dealing with stubborn screws**

Increase the turning power: Screw heads often get so rusty or stripped out the bit can't get a solid hold. Instead of cranking away with the screwdriver bit, clamp a pair of locking pliers onto the screwdriver shaft. Press firmly on the screwdriver and turn the pliers.

Deepen the phillips head: If that doesn't work, drill a 1/8-inch hole into the center of a phillips head. This sometimes allows the tip of a screwdriver to bite in and grab.

Cut the screw: If you have access to the area below, cut through the shank of the screw using a reciprocating saw equipped with a metal-cutting blade.

REPAIRING FRAMING

If you find several framing members that are substantially rotten, it's time to consider tearing down the deck and starting over. However, if the boards are not severely damaged, or if you are certain that only a few are rotten, repairs may solve the problems. Consult with a professional deck builder if you are not sure.

Keeping it strong

If a deck feels spongy when you jump on it, it may be underbuilt, with joists or beams that are too small for their spans *(pages 22–23)*. If you have room to work underneath, it may be possible to shore up a weak deck by installing a new beam with posts and footings. However, this is slow, tedious work. To add a modest amount of extra strength, install a row of blocking in the middle of the joists run *(page 93)* and support it with a post or two.

PRESTART CHECKLIST

☐ **TIME**
A couple of hours for most repairs

☐ **TOOLS**
Drill, hammer, circular saw, reciprocating saw, flat pry bar, cat's paw

☐ **SKILLS**
Fastening with screws or nails while working in awkward positions

☐ **PREP**
Inspect the entire deck to make sure the repairs will fix all the problems

☐ **MATERIALS**
Joist material, 2×4 for braces, screws, nails, carriage bolts with nuts and washers

A. Railing repairs

Damaged cap railing

1 If a cap railing is partially rotten but mostly sound, clean out the joints where moisture and debris collect, let the piece dry, and apply sealer. If the damage is severe, remove the cap and use it as a template for cutting a replacement piece.

2 When installing the new piece of cap railing, begin at a corner joint. Clamp a scrap in place to hold the old and new pieces even. Drill pilot holes before using a 3-inch screw to snug up the joint. Apply two fasteners at each post.

Shoring up a joist

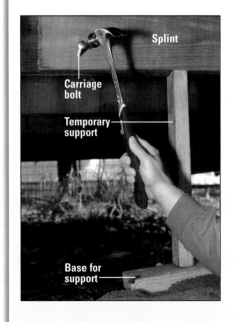

Splint

Carriage bolt

Temporary support

Base for support

A joist that is cracked and sagging can be splinted with a piece of pressure-treated lumber of the same size. Begin by placing a scrap of 2× or a couple of layers of plywood on the ground beneath the damage. Cut a 2×4 long enough to be wedged beneath the joist—it should be long enough to require a few whacks with a hammer to get it nearly upright. Cut a splint so it extends 2 feet on either side of the damage and set it in place above the support. Continue to tap the support upright until the cracked joist ceases to sag and is even with the splint.

Fix the splint in place by drilling holes for two ½×8-inch galvanized carriage bolts at each end. Pound the carriage bolts in place, attach the washer and nut, and tighten.

B. Post repairs

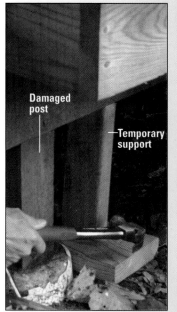

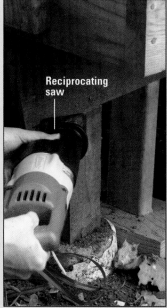

1 Before removing a damaged deck post, install a temporary support to hold up the deck while you work. Lay a 2×6 or 2×8 on the ground below. Cut a 2×4 or 4×4 to fit tightly and hammer it into place.

2 Remove fasteners or cut through them using a reciprocating saw equipped with a metal-cutting blade.

3 Use the old post as a template for cutting a new one. Mimic any notches and angle cuts precisely.

4 Slip the new post into position and fasten it with deck screws, lag screws, or carriage bolts.

Repairing a stringer

1 Stringers often develop rot in the open grain where they were cut. To remove one, take off the posts, railing, and treads. Remove or cut through the nails or screws that hold the stringer in place.

2 Remove the stringer. Lay it on top of a new pressure-treated 2×12, crown side up. Use the old stringer as a template for cutting the new one.

3 Anchor the new stringer securely. Attach it with angle brackets and check for square. Reinstall the treads using 3-inch deck screws.

4 Take the opportunity to replace any damaged stair railing and posts—some may split in the process of dismantling the stairs. Use the old pieces as guides for cutting the new.

APPLYING A FINISH

Home centers offer a wide array of deck cleaners, sealers, and finishes. Check with deck owners in your area to see which products work best and how often they need to be applied. If the deck is exposed to hot sun for extended periods, you may need to apply a fresh coat of sealer every year.

A deck that has turned gray can usually be made to look like new if you wash it and apply a finish. Even grayish-green pressure-treated wood can be stained to resemble cedar or redwood.

It may be worth the cost to hire a professional to finish or refinish your deck. Look through your phone directory for companies that restore, finish, and maintain a deck's appearance. Check out their prices and examine some of the decks they have worked on. Compare the cost with the time and expense it will take you to do it yourself.

PRESTART CHECKLIST

☐ **TIME**
Several hours to clean, and several hours to apply a finish the next day

☐ **TOOLS**
Scrub brush, pressure washer, pole sander, pump sprayer, paintbrush

☐ **SKILLS**
Attention to detail, applying a smooth coat of finish

☐ **PREP**
Consult with a supplier to find the best products for your wood and your climate

☐ **MATERIALS**
Deck cleaner, deck sealer and/or finish

Pole sander

1 Lightly sand the deck using a pole sander, then sweep it thoroughly. Mix a batch of deck cleaner according to manufacturer's directions, apply it, and scrub with a stiff brush.

2 Use a garden hose or a power washer to rinse the cleaner completely from the deck. If you use a power washer, use the fan or 40-degree nozzle. Be careful not to hold the nozzle too close to the wood; the pressure spray can damage the surface.

FINISH INGREDIENTS AND THEIR USES

Choose a finish that contains all the ingredients you need: water repellent to seal out moisture; preservative to protect against mildew, wet rot, and insects; and UV blockers to stop the sun from turning the wood gray.

Finish	Uses
Clear sealers	These products use oil or waxes to keep moisture from soaking in. Some contain preservatives to keep away bugs and prevent mildew.
Semi-transparent stain	Though some products claim to block UV rays without adding color to the wood, the only reliable way to avoid damage from the sun is to add at least a slight pigment. Some finishes dramatically change the color, while others are more subtle.
Resinous finish	This typically comes in two parts and is expensive. The resin gives a deck a permanent wet look. It provides superior protection against water, but may need to be reapplied every year.
Solid stain and porch and deck paint	A solid stain completely changes the color of a board, but allows its grain to show through. Paint covers the color and texture of a board. Oil-based products can be long lasting; latex-based products will wear away quickly.

3 Allow the deck to dry completely. Use a pump sprayer to spread sealer/stain onto the deck. Cover a strip about 3 feet wide— an easy reach for brushing.

4 Immediately brush the surface with a 5- to 6-inch brush so there will be no puddles. Move the brush in one direction only, always with the grain.

5 For detail work, use a smaller brush. Pay attention to the edges of boards, so you don't end up with brush strokes that run across the grain.

STANLEY PRO TIP: **Rent a power washer**

Use a power washer to clean a deck with water only or use it to rinse a deck after scrubbing with deck cleaner. Be sure to use a nozzle that fans out; a focused spray can create dents and carve channels, especially in soft cedar or redwood.

Apply with a roller

A simple paint roller can be used instead of a pump sprayer. Work carefully to avoid blobs and streaks. Brush the wood within a couple minutes of applying with the roller.

GLOSSARY

For terms not included here, or for more about those that are, refer to the index on *pages 118–120.*

Baluster: The smaller vertical members of a railing system, which are usually spaced at regular intervals between posts.

Batterboard: Made of two approximately 18-inch stakes and an approximately 24-inch crosspiece, a batterboard supports layout strings to pinpoint the location of piers.

Beam: A large horizontal framing piece, usually made of 4× or doubled 2× lumber, which usually rests on posts and is used to support joists.

Bevel cut: An angle cut through the thickness of a piece of wood.

Blocking: Short pieces of lumber, usually the same dimension as the joists, cut to fit between joists. Blocking prevents the warping of joists and adds strength.

Bubble plan: A plan that includes such nonstructural considerations as view, landscaping features, and traffic patterns.

Building codes: Community ordinances governing the manner in which a home may be constructed or modified. Most codes are primarily concerned with fire and health, with separate sections relating to electrical, plumbing, and structural work.

Building permit: A license authorizing specified new construction. The permit requires that the work be done in accordance with building codes and requires one or more inspections. In most municipalities, building a deck requires a building permit.

Butt joint: The joint formed by two pieces of material cut at 90 degrees when fastened end to end, end to face, or end to edge.

Cantilever: A member that extends beyond a post, typically more than 2 feet. Cantilevers shorten the span between posts and help hide some posts, giving the deck the appearance of floating.

Check: A crack on the surface of a board. If the check runs more than halfway through the thickness of a board, structural integrity is diminished and the board should not be used.

Cleat: A length of board attached to strengthen or add support to a structure.

Countersink: To drive the head of a nail or screw so that its top is flush with the surface of the surrounding wood.

Crook: A bend along the length of a board, visible by sighting along one edge. With decking, a slight crook—no more than ¾ inch in an 8-foot board—can be corrected when the board is installed.

Crosscut: To saw lumber perpendicular to its length and/or its grain.

Crown: A slight edgewise bow in a board. In framing, the crown edge is placed upward so gravity will, in time, force it down.

Cup: A curve across the width of a board is a cup. Unless it is severe, cupping is not a problem for framing lumber. In a decking board, slight cupping can be taken out by screwing down each side of the board. Reject any boards with cupping more than ⅜ inch deep.

Decking: The boards used to make the walking surface of a deck. Decking is usually made of 2×6, 2×4, or ⅝×6 lumber.

Elevation drawing: This plan shows the vertical face of a deck, emphasizing footings, posts, railings, and any built-in planters, benches, skirting, or overhead structures.

End grain: The ends of wood fibers, exposed at the ends of boards.

Finial: An ornament attached to the top of a post or the peak of an arch.

Flashing: Bent strips of sheet metal, usually galvanized steel or aluminum, that protect lumber from water. On a deck, flashing is often used to protect the ledger and the sheathing behind it.

Flush: On the same plane, or level with, the surrounding or adjacent surface.

Footing: A small foundation, usually of concrete, that supports a post. See *Pier.*

Frost heave: The upthrust of soil caused when moist soil freezes. Posts and footings that do not extend below the frost line are subject to frost heave.

Frost line: The maximum depth at which the ground in your area freezes during winter.

Grade: The surface of the ground.

Grading: Altering the surface of ground to permit drainage, prepare an area for a stair landing, and generally smooth the ground near a structure.

Header joist: Set at a right angle to inside joists, the header joist is a perimeter joist to which inside joists are attached. Header joists always run parallel to major beams and ledgers.

Heartwood:. The center and most durable part of a tree, often marked by a deeper color than the surrounding wood.

Joist: Horizontal framing members that support a floor and/or ceiling. An *inside* or *common* joist is a nonperimeter joist.

Joist hanger: A metal piece of connector used to join a joist and a ledger or rim joist so that their top edges are flush.

Lag screw: A screw, usually ¼ inch in diameter or larger, with a hexagonal head that can be driven with a wrench or socket.

Lattice: A horizontal surface made of crisscrossed pieces of wood or vinyl.

Ledger: A horizontal strip (typically lumber) that's used to provide support for the ends or edges of other members.

Level: The condition that exists when any type of surface is at true horizontal. Also a tool used to determine level.

Miter joint: The joint that is formed when two members meet that have been cut at the same angle (usually 45 degrees).

Nominal dimension: The stated size of a piece of lumber, such as a 2×4 or a 1×12. The actual dimension is slightly smaller.

On-center (OC): A phrase used to designate the distance from the center of one regularly spaced framing member to the center of the next.

Outside joist: A joist that is part of the perimeter framing structure, other than a ledger, of a deck.

Pergola: An open overhead structure designed to provide shade and/or to support hanging or climbing plants.

Pier: A vertical piece of concrete, used as a footing to support a post. A pier can be poured concrete, or a ready-made concrete pier. See *Footing.*

Pilot hole: A small hole drilled into a wooden member to avoid splitting the wood when driving a screw or nail.

Plan-view drawing: An overhead view of a deck, which shows locations of footings and framing members.

Plumb: The condition that exists when a member is at true vertical. See *Level.*

Plunge cut: A cut made with a circular saw where the blade is brought into contact with the wood from above to avoid continuing the cut to an edge or end of a board.

Post: This vertical framing piece, usually 4×4 or 6×6, is used to support a beam or a joist.

Pressure-treated wood: Lumber and sheet goods impregnated with one of several solutions (typically chromated copper arsenate) to make the wood virtually impervious to moisture and weather.

Rafter: In deck building, a framing member that supports the uppermost material that makes up a pergola.

Rail: A horizontal framing member of railing that spans between posts to support balusters and sometimes the cap rail.

Rim joist: A term sometimes used to describe an outside joist.

Rip: To saw lumber or sheet goods parallel to its grain pattern.

Rise: The total vertical distance a stairway climbs. Also, the vertical distance between the topmost surface of two sequential treads.

Riser: A board attached to the vertical cut surface of a stair stringer, used to cover up the gap between treads and to provide some additional tread support.

Run: The total horizontal distance a stairway spans from the structure to finished grade level. Also, the horizontal depth of a tread cut made in a stringer.

Sapwood: The lighter-colored, more recent growth of any species of wood used as lumber.

Sealant: A protective coating (usually clear) applied to wood and metal.

Setback: The minimum distance between a property line and any structure, as delimited by local building departments.

Shim: A thin strip or wedge of wood or other material used to fill a gap between two adjoining components or to help establish level or plumb.

Site plan: A map of your property, showing where the deck will be located on your yard.

Skirt or skirting: Horizontal pieces of lumber installed around the perimeter of a deck to screen the area below the deck. Skirting may be made of vertical or horizontal solid boards, or it may be made of lattice.

Span: The distance traveled by a beam, joist, or decking board between supporting structures.

Square: The condition that exists when one surface is at a 90-degree angle to another.

Stringer: A diagonal board used to support treads and risers on a stairway. Stringers are usually made of 2×12s.

3–4–5 method: An easy, mathematical way to check whether a large angle is square. Measure 3 feet along one side, and 4 feet along the other; if the corner is square, the diagonal distance between those two points will equal 5 feet.

Toe-fasten: To drive a screw or nail at an angle when joining a piece where head-on fastening is not possible.

Wane: The rounded-off corner along the edge of a board, where there once was bark.

INDEX

METRIC CONVERSIONS

U.S. Units to Metric Equivalents			Metric Units to U.S. Equivalents		
To convert from	Multiply by	To get	To convert from	Multiply by	To get
Inches	25.4	Millimeters	Millimeters	0.0394	Inches
Inches	2.54	Centimeters	Centimeters	0.3937	Inches
Feet	30.48	Centimeters	Centimeters	0.0328	Feet
Feet	0.3048	Meters	Meters	3.2808	Feet
Yards	0.9144	Meters	Meters	1.0936	Yards
Square inches	6.4516	Square centimeters	Square centimeters	0.1550	Square inches
Square feet	0.0929	Square meters	Square meters	10.764	Square feet
Square yards	0.8361	Square meters	Square meters	1.1960	Square yards
Acres	0.4047	Hectares	Hectares	2.4711	Acres
Cubic inches	16.387	Cubic centimeters	Cubic centimeters	0.0610	Cubic inches
Cubic feet	0.0283	Cubic meters	Cubic meters	35.315	Cubic feet
Cubic feet	28.316	Liters	Liters	0.0353	Cubic feet
Cubic yards	0.7646	Cubic meters	Cubic meters	1.308	Cubic yards
Cubic yards	764.55	Liters	Liters	0.0013	Cubic yards

To convert from degrees Fahrenheit (F) to degrees Celsius (C), first subtract 32, then multiply by ⅝.

To convert from degrees Celsius to degrees Fahrenheit, multiply by ⅘, then add 32.